When Cancer Knocks at Your Door

FIGHT. PRAY. SLAY.

Presented by LaDonna Stanley-Thompson

Foreword by LaSonji Holman-Cole, CFNP, MSN, BSN

Copyright © **2025 by LaDonna Stanley-Thompson**

Cover Design by LaDonna Stanley-Thompson & LaKesha L. Williams

All Rights Reserved. No part of this publication may be reproduced, stored in a retrieval system, or transmitted in any form or by any means, electronic, mechanical, photocopying or otherwise, without the prior written permission of the copyright owner. If you would like permission to use material from the book (other than for review purposes), please contact mymelegacy223@gmail.com. Thank you for your support of authors' rights.

ISBN: 979-8-218-50779-4

Published by The VTF Collective, a Hybrid Publishing House

(www.TheVTFCollective.com)

First Edition (April) 2025

The VTF Collective

ALL RIGHTS RESERVED

PRINTED IN THE USA

All Scripture quotations are public domain courtesy of Bible Gateway: www.Biblegateway.com

Contents

Dedication
Special Thanks
Acknowledgements
Foreword   7

Poem: The Unexpected Gift
    Txny T   8

Part 1: The Unexpected Gift
    LaDonna Stanley-Thompson   14

Part 2: Three Battles, One Warrior
    Desiree Waters   43

Part 3: When the Highway of Happiness Forces You to Take an Unexpected Detour
    Karen Hargrove   96

Part 4: Cancer!? Never Crossed My Mind
    DeWayne Perry   116

Part 5: Atomic Prayers
    Kenyette Spencer   130

Dedication

This book is dedicated to my beautiful mother **Martha Vestoria Stanley** who taught me how to fight by keeping my eyes fixed on Jesus. She was truly a warrior for Christ and overcame so many challenges in her life, but she never let those challenges stop her from succeeding in life or in God. She also showed me the importance of keeping family and friends close because we all need somebody to lean on.

To my beautiful mentors who are now my angels: **Bobbie Smith** and **Barbara Brown**. They won the fight against cancer and are now with our Lord and Savior.

To my beautiful sister/friend **Bambi Richardson** who showed me how to show up for a friend regardless of the circumstance. May she continue to sleep in peace.

Special Thanks To

To my Lord and Savior Jesus Christ, my wonderful husband Anthony Thompson, Sr. (aka Tony), my beautiful son Anthony Thompson, Jr. (aka AJ), my dear sister Deneane Stanley, my sister/friends LaSonji Holman and Carla Thomas.

Dr. Gamble, Dr. Caiseda, Pastor and Lady Poullard, my family, my Fort Washington Baptist Church (FWBC) family, my Federal Aviation Administration (FAA) co-workers/colleagues/friends and Federal Aviation Christina Fellowship (FACF) family, my friends, ancestors, my co-authors, Coach Kesha and VTF Publishing Company.

Remember, when cancer knocks at your door, love shows up right after it.

It is a gift because you now know something that you did not know before, and you can address it no matter how challenging it may be. It is also a gift because although it's a diagnosis, you are still on this side of heaven and have a little more time to spend with family and friends.

Acknowledgements

LaSonji Holman

Deneane Stanley

Dr. Gamble

Dr. Caiseda

Pastor and Lady Poulard

Family

FWBC Family

Friends

Ancestors

My Co-Authors

Roxanne Young

Coach Kesha

Foreword

Cancer is a gift – WHAT? In my 30 years of practice as a Nurse Practitioner, I have never heard of cancer described in this way. The word cancer is associated with very negative connotations and has been likened by some to a thief, a demon, or a murderer. Conversely, the word gift invokes excitement, anticipation and happiness. So, describing cancer as a gift sounds very paradoxical. But given the source of this description, my ever-optimistic, larger than life sister-friend LaDonna Stanley-Thompson, I was not surprised. LaDonna's life is rooted in the knowledge that God our Father gives us good and perfect gifts.

As you read the gripping and very transparent testimonies of the cancer survivors in this book, you will feel their pain, their worries, and their fears, their setbacks, challenges and struggles. Regardless of the type of cancer, the path toward healing is not easy. This journey is very complex and riddled with unexpected twists and turns. However, you will also feel strengthened by their courage and enlightened by their insights and pearls of wisdom. You see, the difficult experiences are intertwined with love, joy, peace beyond understanding, and faith in the immutable power of God.

My prayer is that those who read this book will be inspired to view their own journeys of cancer or any other major life challenge that comes knocking through the lens of my beautiful friend, LaDonna – as a gift.

LaSonji Holman-Cole, CFNP, MSN, BSN

The Unexpected Gift

From the heart of the author's son

Txny T

What kinda gift is this

God never mentioned this

I didn't wish for this

Feeling numb, sick and pissed

We pray for the families that go through this pain

And yet God saw fit to let me experience the same

Looks towards the past to see what could have been changed

And thoughts towards my future now seem out of range

The wave of change running through my life, work,

finances and health are now all unknown

Life's at a dull tone

Family seeing the obstacles ahead,

not sure if they can be relied on

But I fight on

Friends seeming to become further out of reach,

contact squeezed thin, as if wrapped by a python

It hasn't even been long

Feeling alone, trapped, misunderstood, defeated

Laying in my bed literally singing sad songs

My joy is gone

If only Cancer was a person, I swear I would beat his a*

What if I could get my hands on depression, I'd f*** him up

And don't let anxiety be there, cuz I'd double up

I can forget such and such

The whispers from those looking to see what they can gain

The vultures around me, watching my demise, to feed themselves,

but to them it's all the same

I'm falling into a dark place

Experiencing this heart ache

Surrounded by mannequins

My friends are all fake

I've made too many mistakes

But to think I deserved a "gift" like this

Is a hot take

And to think my God proclaimed this to be a gift,

and I would never question the Most High,

But for this to be a gift, why must someone die?

Who knew that this test, at this time, would be meant for me

And instantly

I'm reminded that I don't lean on myself in hard times, well silly me

I look up to the heavens proclaiming that only God's will, will be

Iron sharpens iron, and I will have my blade polished until my shine's pristine.

He surrounds me with those who share my pain

Those that overcame

My heart needs maintenance, and He gave me patience

And the courage to go on against anything I'm faced with.

God gave me the gift of pain,

To surround me with the people who have been healed

God gave me the gift of struggle, so I can truly enjoy the feeling to succeed

God gave me the gift of numbness, for me to appreciate what I feel

God gave me the gift of a test, so that I can prove to all that see my journey, that my God is REAL.

The Unexpected Gift

From the heart of the author's son

TO HEAR POEM

by Txny T

STORIES OF FAITH COURAGE AND RESILIENCE

Part 1:

The Unexpected Gift

by LaDonna Stanley-Thompson

The Unexpected Gift

LaDonna Stanley-Thompson

The year 2023 was one for the books! Well one thing about life is that it is full of surprises. This year for me was full of so many exciting activities with family, friends, community, ministry, and work. I am not a person who consistently journals, so I try to capture important events on Facebook so that I can have somewhere besides my cell phone photo gallery to look back on. If I was to describe this year with one word, I would say it was "exceptional." I was grinding in every area of my life. It almost seemed as if I had supernatural strength to do so and when I recount the many activities that I was physically involved with, it indeed was a supernatural power carrying me.

I'm listing below the events in bullet format to give you an idea of my schedule.

• The hubby and I went on our annual Valentine Marriage retreat in Williamsburg, VA.

• My big sister Deneane and I celebrated my mom by going to a Golden Girls Performance at the Warner Theatre.

• I took my husband to Myrtle Beach for his birthday. This was the first time the airline lost our luggage. We didn't get it back until a few days after returning home. We had a ball despite the loss of the luggage. We ate at Paula Deen's restaurant for the first time...OMG! It was divine!

• I attended more than 10 significant milestone birthday celebrations.

LaDonna Stanley-Thompson

- I attended at least 10 events at the Kennedy Center.

- I traveled out of state at least 5 times: including traveling out of the country in November.

- I had at least 30 lunch/dinner dates regarding business and personal matters.

- I attended at least 4 musical events at the Birchmere with my hubby, family and friends. At one of these concerts, I heard Victory Boyd for the first time, and it was as if I heard an angel singing. I booked her for one of my church events and for a SHoLOVE event this same year: with less than 24 hours between each event.

- I got an unexpected promotion on my job.

- I got an unexpected STEM Award on my job.

- My son moved back home (I orchestrated the move) along with his 2 one year old German Shepherds.

- I went to the Naval Academy Gospel Concert with my sister-friend Jacqueline.

- I saw Comedian Jon Christ at the Capital One Arena with a sister/friend.

- We had Couples Date Night with friends at Bridgeway Community Church featuring comedian Michael Jr. in the "Marriage Works Tour."

LaDonna Stanley-Thompson

- My son AJ and I went to support a sister-friend, Kandace, in a theatrical performance called "Diagnosed" at Creative Cauldron.

- I saw CeCe Winans in person twice at her "Believe for It Tour": Once with my sister-friends on a road trip and once with the hubby at the Kennedy Center.

- I had several intentional lunch/dinner dates with my 25-year-old son AJ.

- I attended my 1st born niece Andrea's college graduation at UNCG. She completed this task having a full-time job, mothering 5 children, being a wife and being active in ministry at her church.

- My god-daughter Janella surprised me for Mother's Day and came to my church.

- I saw Mrs. Christi at Funny Bone in Richmond with Hubby. My sister Deneane and her friend surprised me and came from NC to the show.

- My neighbor Telicia and Winslow got married in Greenville, NC that same weekend Andrea graduated, and the hubby and I attended both events. I'm still tired!

- We had a successful FWBC Revival and Homecoming Day with the theme "Level Up"

- I celebrated 5 years of marriage with the hubby by having dinner at Fogo de Chao and seeing the Lion King Show at the Kennedy Center.

- We had a successful Scholarship Brunch Wars Fundraiser event for SHoLOVE.

- We lost one of my mother's best friends: Mrs. Betty Sanker, she was a jewel.

- My big sister Barbara and my nephew Siefyan came down from New York to stay with me for a few days. They were a blessing.

- I turned 54 on my birthday and traveled to Atlantic City for a get-away.

- I went to Dallas Texas to attend the Woman Evolve Conference. My big sister Deneane and my 2 nieces, Andrea and Jen, attended also. The entire time both being there with family and at the conference was life-changing. We registered for 2025 already.

- My big sister and I did a last-minute trip to Toronto. I want to move there.

- My sister-friend and ministry partner organized a Sneaker Gala at our Church (FWBC) featuring Victory Boyd. What a wonderful event! Also, SHoLOVE, in collaboration with Mothers of Black Boys (MOBB), had a "Prayer for our Sons" brunch at the Harborside Hotel featuring Victory Boyd. What a wonderful event!

- I went to a Samara Joy Christmas concert at the Strathmore with my sister/friend Carla.

I had to capture all those things in writing just so you can understand why I said this year was one for the books! I mean, up until the last major event I was responsible for leading. Then my body said ENOUGH.

Your Body Will Give You Signs That Something Is Wrong (FIGHT. PRAY. SLAY.)

I had been trying to get to the bottom of why I was bleeding so heavily and constantly for 3 years with no resolve. If you do not have a tough stomach, skip this section. Let me explain to you the type of bleeding I had. I would bleed heavily for at least 25 days out of the month. I would go through the large purple Always pads (27 count) in a couple of days. I owned about 50 pairs of underwear. It was normal for me to pass clots the size of a grape (diameter of a quarter). I could easily go through 2 pads within 1 hour and after I showered and got dressed for work, I would have to sometimes change my clothes due to the extensive and fast bleeding. I would have to carry 2 sets of clothes with me in a backpack in case an accident occurred. When I traveled, I always made sure I had at least 2 packs of the 27 count Always pads with me. I could ONLY wear the purple ones. There was so much blood expelling from my body that I would often say to myself: How do I still have blood left in me? Many times, I would have to put a towel or bag under me while driving and while sleeping. I was an absolute bloody mess. But, with all that, I learned to maneuver and deal with it because all the pap smears would come back normal. This way of life became my norm. My former gynecologist said that it was me going through perimenopause. Yep, I was in perimenopause for 10 years!

Finally, my new gynecologist did advise me to schedule a surgery for a biopsy and I delayed scheduling it. By the time I scheduled it as an in and out surgery, I went to get my blood drawn for the pre-op so that they could ensure I was able to go under anesthesia. The next day my results came back. My doctor called me on a Friday while I was at work and asked me how I was feeling. I said I feel okay. I am a little tired. He said: Well, I am going to ask you to go directly to the ER because your blood level is in a critical zone, and you can collapse at any time. He said do not drive yourself and go directly to the hospital. When I got there and told them what my doctor said, they immediately took me, put me in a room, drew my blood and told me it was at a 5. They ordered 2 pints so that I would at least get to a 7. I was told then that most people have 10 to 13 pints of blood in their bodies. After receiving the blood, I immediately started feeling better. The racing of my heart that had become the norm to me for about 3 months subsided. I did not know that was a sign of my blood level being so low.

After this ordeal, I muscled up the courage to do the in-office procedure for the biopsy. I asked my sister-friend and Nurse Practitioner LaSonjito accompany me and she did. I had the procedure on Friday, December 29, 2023. I received the diagnosis Friday, January 5, 2024. Dr. Caiseda called that evening and said: "LaDonna, I hate to call you with this news, but the biopsy shows that you have a form of cancer, and it's called endometrial adenocarcinoma. The good news is that it can be treated with surgery. I am now referring you to a gynecologic oncologist that will take care of that for you and her name is Dr. Gamble."

The Prayers of the Righteous Avails Much (FIGHT. PRAY. SLAY.)

My first appointment with the gynecologic oncologist was Jan.17, 2024. Planning for this day was very emotional. I initially said I was going to go alone so that I did not have to deal with anyone feeling sorry for me. Then when I told my sister/friend she immediately said: "Oh no, you cannot! It is critical that you take someone with you because you are going to be too emotional to remember things that were said, so you need someone that will take notes." Well, I knew I could not depend on the hubby to take good notes, so I invited my niece Andrea to join me via telecon and that was the best thing I could have done. I was not professionally prepared when I went in, but my niece took notes like she was a professional scriber, and she asked questions like I was the most precious gem in the room and had to ensure all care instructions were clear. Even my doctor said those were great questions. The hubby was there to hug me when I did get a little emotional.

When I first met my oncologist Dr. Charlotte Gamble, I said to myself that she is so young. She was wearing a mask so I did not get a full picture of her, but I could tell she was young. Her professionalism was 5-star. Her bedside manners made me feel so at ease. I felt like a great auntie that she was going to make sure understood everything. She pulled out an 8x11 pamphlet that had clear pictures of the body part that was cancerous. She circled, noted and verbally explained both everything that was going on with me and what would be done to manage and remove the cancer. I do not ever recall receiving this level of professionalism and care: to the extent that I left her office hopeful and ready to conquer Goliath.

Emotional Triggers (FIGHT. PRAY. SLAY.)

One of the biggest things that saddens me is the look in my son's eyes when I talk about the diagnosis. He walks away or says: "Please, Mom!" He says, "I can't bear the thought of losing you." I know what he is feeling because I felt the same way about my mom. My prayer is: "Lord, give my son renewed strength. Help him seek Your face, not just for this situation, but for all situations, in Jesus Name." Your attitude determines your altitude. So, in the words of Karlton Humes, who uses the social media handle @NotKarltonBanks, #FaithCancer. Please look him up on social media and see how he uses the word "faith."

At any given moment, tears will fall just because. Let them fall and acknowledge that you are not weak, but you're a human with emotions. I had just started reading Dr. Anita Phillips book "The Garden Within" and when I tell you all I did was cry while reading every chapter because each one was so relatable.

SIDE NOTE: Make appointments ASAP so that there is no delay in treatment.

Some people will not know what to say. Some may offend you with what they say, and some may offend you when they don't say anything. It's a journey that can be new and challenging to/for family, friends, colleagues, associates, and enemies. Yes Girl, your enemy is not going to know how to act. They are not going to know whether to call you or to send you either a card, flowers or food. They are not even going to know how to "prey" for you! LOL! Only focus on the things that are important and don't be distracted by the awkward nuances. By all means, surround yourself with positive and mature minded people. Don't get distracted when negative people cross your path. Recognize them immediately and refocus on the goal (your physical and emotional stability). Don't get flustered with thinking about life and what you would have loved to accomplish. Be grateful for what you have already accomplished. Focus on your health and the journey ahead: one minute at a time.

As previously mentioned, my dear sister-friend and ministry partner, LaSonji, is a nurse practitioner and Big God divinely connected us because He knew this would be part of my journey. She told me that I should only be focusing on my health because I would need every single bit of strength and energy to get through this. She was so gentle telling me this, but I knew she had her own concerns because she loves me as a sister in Christ. I listened and put everything on the back burner. That was one of the most important instructions I received.

BREATHE DEEP, inhale through your nose and exhale slowly through your mouth. Go ahead. Try it this very moment and do it 5 times and see how better you will feel. See! Yes, it really is a good stress releaser.

Ecclesiastes 3 is one of my favorite chapters in the Bible. I was led to focus on not only that chapter, but the whole book of Ecclesiastes. Time belongs to God. Focus on your healing and

He will restore the time the locust (cancer) has stolen. God is still in control regardless of the report. Don't stop dreaming your biggest dreams and don't stop planning for your next business and pleasurable venture. I am one that plans my trips and concerts 6 months to a year in advance. I had several trips and date nights set up for me and the hubby. I was sad when I had to cancel them, but I spoke life to myself and said there will be another time.

You are going to experience a lot of first times: first time to ever be sick, first time to feel like closing your eyes and hoping this is just a dream, first time completing the health intake form and checking off a major illnesses, first time getting a CT Scan, first time having to be vulnerable to loved ones, first time having to take off work for more than 2 weeks, first time solely caring about yourself...you get the picture.

My first entry to document the journey was Sunday, January 21, 2024. I picked up my phone and created a contact name (the title of my book): "When Cancer Knocks at Your Door." I then started the notes under that contact. My first entry was "You will feel lonely, but you are never alone." I referenced Psalms 116. Pastor preached from Psalms 116 that day: specifically for the saints (me included) that are going through. Part of the message he explained is it's not a sin to pray for more time on earth. That message spoke to me and redirected my thinking. I had already vowed that I was okay with going to see Jesus because this life was not all peaches and cream anyway; however, after the message I had a change of heart. Everyone will have his/her own way of dealing with their journey. Some will do it with just a friend or two. Some will have a village. Some will have a community. Some will have the world. I choose to do it with God, family, my church and my village. After I typed these entries, I checked to see if there was a book titled "When Cancer Knocks at Your Door" and guess what, it was clear that was the book God gave to me to write because I couldn't find one with that title! Come on here, Big God! Do your thang!

I've been a professional and natural caregiver to/for my mom, my spiritual mentors (Bobbie and Barbara), and to my friend Bambi. I was strong for them. When you sow strength into others, your family and friends are going to be strong for you. You reap what you sow. Let me tell you something, I prayed that my reaping would be good and not be a lesson LOL! When you awake every morning, pause to say "Thank You, God for waking me up this morning. Give me strength to get through this day."

Take care of business **ASAP**. Family matters. Keep the family as updated as possible of your appointments and certain business you are responsible for. Ensure all your life insurance policies are in active status. If you don't have life insurance, get it or at least get a burial plan through the funeral home. If you are unable to do that at least let your family and friends know that you do not have anything in place. This is also a good time to jot down some of your last will and testaments and give it to a responsible family member, friend or colleague. Inform your family who has your last will and testament document and be sure it is notarized. Be sure that the notary contact information is attached with the document. If possible, get a will so that way it is documented with a lawyer and filed with the courts and cannot be changed.

Every Day is a New Day (Jan. 25, 2024) A very famous man once said "Life is like a box of chocolates. You never know what you're gonna' get!" You also never know where your next wind will come from or who it will come from. I had a missed call from my college. They then sent a text message asking me to enroll asap before I go inactive. I called the number back and the system directed me to a representative. I could tell she was an older Caucasian woman. I asked her to please put on my account that I have been diagnosed with cancer and I will not be enrolling anytime soon. The representative immediately went into mother mode. She said "Let me go on this other topic. I just went through that, and I am on the other side of it now. So just know you will get through it." She said, "I am not gonna lie to you, chemo is hard, but you will get through it." I immediately responded to every encouragement with a yes, Mam. She then said: "If you are a godly woman just ask God to put you in places where you can talk about God" and she then said, "Remember this is not a punishment, but a test of your faith." The tears started falling and my voice started trembling more and more while I am saying yes Mam. She said: "You're going to be okay" and then she said "Just focus on taking care of you and I will get this message to the administrator to put in your files. Take care now!" While recapturing this event, it still makes me cry. The empathy she expressed to me was so warm and so needed. Your journey is your journey. It was designed specifically for you. God will be your helper...one day at a time...one hour at a time...one minute at a time...one second at a time...one moment at a time!

The Importance of Sister/Friends (Jan. 26, 2024) My sister/friend LaSonji, who has also been my life saver, constantly reminds me that God made sure I would be surrounded by love during this process. I so feel the love and I am truly grateful. Okay, I am about to take y'all to church, again! I watched, on YouTube, the first 2024 "Hey You" service with Sarah Jakes Roberts and the speaker was Dr. Anita Phillips. In her message she said (I am paraphrasing because I had to write fast) "Get your hands off. Get away from it. Get your mind off. God does things while you are resting. Mark 4. The day begins when I have fully rested. God was working while you were sleeping. God sees your need, so go to sleep! Yes, Jesus! The wisdom of God! Rest! Rest! Rest! Just lay down like Jacob. The rest don't even have to be comfortable. Stop trying to be the generational breaker in your family. Lay down your burdens. While you are sleeping, needs will be met! In Jesus Name!"

Not only did I have sisters praying for me, but I also had my natural and spiritual brothers praying for me. It touched my heart when my husband's best friend called me and said "I'm praying for you, and I fasted for you, and I have never fasted before. I told the Lord: "You can't take her" and He said to me "It's just a test to make her stronger and to get our attention." Then He said, "You are going to be alright, Sis!"

One of my mentors told me talk to people that have gone through a similar situation to prepare as best possible. OMG!

That was the best advice! I was so surprised when I found out how many women have had a partial and/or a full hysterectomy.

On Saturday, January 27, 2024, I had been staying low key and at home most of the time trying to get the house prepared for the big surgery day. I wanted the home to be as comfortable as possible and easy for the 2 men in my life to maintain. They stress me out keeping the house messy when I am well so I knew that would be a trigger for me. However, I had been planning since October for the hubby and I to attend this Marriage Master Class given by Evangel Cathedral with Apostle Don Meares, so we cleaned ourselves up and had a date. It was so needed and so worth it. It was a 6.5-hour lecture session, and I was so proud of the hubby, I only had to nudge him one time. He was very engaged. It felt like a retreat for us. God knew we needed it. The hubby said to me "Babe, I want this for us" and I said, "Me too." Come through, Jesus!

January is Cervical Cancer Month. WOW! (Jan. 31, 2024) I went for my 2nd visit to my Oncologist so that I could get the results of the CT scan and to get a date for the surgery. The hubby was with me. Dr. Gamble said the CT scan looked great and the date for the surgery will be 2/6/2024. OMG 6 days, OMG! Major surgery in 6 days?! OMG! Dr. Gamble took out time for me and the hubby to ask any questions we had concerning the surgery, and she gave us a breakdown of how the day would go. Oh, and this is so important, when you are having surgery: get your doctor to pre-order all your medications for post-surgery. This made my coming home and healing process so much easier. I never experienced pain above a 3 and I never had to take the narcotics that were prescribed.

When Dr. Gamble explained how I would be positioned during surgery I asked if she could ensure my knees were positioned in a way where they would not get hurt because I had severe arthritis in both and that they could easily dislocate. She made a note and assured me she would make sure they were in a comfortable position. Then she said why haven't you seen an orthopedist about this. I told her I did years ago, but I need to get a new one. She said she knew one. Then she quickly said: "Okay, one thing at a time. Let's get this cancer taken care of and then we will circle back around." Just those words *"circle back around"* were words of hope and healing. That night I wrote in my journal Dr. Gamble is phenomenal!

The caregiving for you starts way before the actual surgery. You are emotionally and physically drained from all the doctor's appointments, the unknowns, the getting things in order on your job and in your home and the mere acceptance of the reality that this is your life. You have cancer and you must address all that comes with it.

Love Overflowing. The Reaping Season (FIGHT. PRAY. SLAY.)

1 day before surgery I did the following:

• Confirmed everything at work was okay

• Made sure all items/medications needed after surgery were ordered (ohhh the stomach pillow was my best friend)

- Cleaned my house/bedroom/kitchen (well, had it cleaned by friends and professionals)

- Had friends come over just for some good laughing and fellowship

- Had a corporate prayer with my sister inner circle

- Took a lot of deep breaths

- Ensured my last will and testament is with the person to carry them out

- Hung up my mother's lounge gown right next to my bed (it was my keepsake and comfort clothing) so that it would be visible when I come home from surgery and recovery. My mother has been gone for 16.5 years now

- Trusted God

Surgery Day Tuesday, February 6, 2024, at 2PM! I got to the hospital at 11:45am and left at 9:15PM.

All the staff were great! From the registration to the pre-op room, to the recovery room, and to the chair taxi personnel that strolled me to my car. I remembered most of their names after surgery: Geme and Ruby (operating room nurse), Dr. Cray (head anesthesiologist with years of experience), and Kathyryn (recovery nurse who cheered for me when I peed, LOL!) Kathryn told me that she prays for all her patients every night and she asked what would I like her to pray for? I said please, please, please pray for me that I will be patient with my husband and pray that my recovery goes well. Prayer works y'all!

When I came home, I was still high from anesthesia. My son and my husband helped me up the 15 steps, and the first thing I saw when I walked in my bedroom was my mother's gown. That's when I broke down with grateful tears. My son said: "Mom what's wrong?" I said: "I am just grateful son, I am just so grateful!" I was home in my own bed! God is good and the drugs are good and my family, my friends, my co-workers and my community are good!

That pain medicine schedule is so important. My schedule was:

7:00 PM Ibuprofen

10:00 PM Tylenol

1:00 AM Ibuprofen

4:00 AM Tylenol

7:00 AM Ibuprofen

10:00 AM Tylenol

1:00 PM Ibuprofen

4:00 PM Tylenol

By following this schedule my pain never got higher than a three and I never had to take the hard stuff (narcotics) that were prescribed.

I told myself I would lose weight during this 12-week healing time, but everybody kept sending me all these fruit and food baskets, dinners, and treats. Lord, Lord, Lord! I want to try it all. Oh my! The flowers, plants, stuffed animals, blankets, cards, money, ginger products, coloring books, and journals were awesome! I needed them all. One of my friends visited me 3 days after surgery and when she walked in my bedroom, she said: "Oh my, this place is starting to look like a funeral home with all these floral arrangements." I had to use my fake laugh because I could not afford to bust any stitches laughing and I did not want to feel the pain. I had learned how to laugh without putting pressure on my stomach muscles.

Speaking of laughing, before surgery I told my sister Deneane and my friend Carla that they cannot do any crazy stuff to make me laugh. We always laugh at everything and always have a story that just comes out of nowhere. My sister was saying well in that case, I can never come in your room because that's all we do. My big sister Deneane stayed with me for 2 weeks and nurtured me back to health. She traveled from NC and came to Maryland 4 days prior to my surgery. When I say I worked her, my husband, my son, my cousin, my friend Carla and Lady Rasheeda Brown like they were being paid, I worked them! They did all that for love. I couldn't afford to pay them their worth anyway. God set it all up for me and I am still very grateful. People do not have to be nice to you, but it's so wonderful when they are.

Beware! You are vulnerable in every aspect (physically, spiritually, and emotionally) of your life (FIGHT. PRAY. SLAY.)

I was unaware of an attack that the devil planned for my sweet niece Gabby (my twin niece). She had a health crisis the day before my surgery, but my very wise sister-in-love Niecy told my sister not to say anything to me so that I would be clear and calm for my surgery. When I did learn about her hospitalization and illness, I was able to pray for her and be calm, because I was in a posture of prayer, healing and covering. We were both in need of prayer and healing.

Some of the healing and covering songs I listened to were:

1. Glory Hour CD by Victory Boyd

2. Through it All by Andrae Crouch

3. Trust Me by Richard Smallwood

4. God is Good by Jonathan McReynolds

5. The Goodness of God by CeCe Winans

6. Good Morning by PJ Morton

7. Grace Mercy and Peace by Brain Courtney Wilson

8. His Eye is on the Sparrow by Victory Boyd

9. Lord You Are Good by Todd Galberth

10. Dear God by Smokie Norful

11. I Believe by Fred Jenkins feat Bishop Paul Morton

12. Overcomer by Mandisa

13. Through the Storm by Yolanda Adams

I did not watch TV for 1.5 weeks. I needed to be in tune with the Lord. I literally rested and healed and enjoyed being able to rest and relax. I really did not know how to do that, and it really felt great. When I finally watched TV, oh my! Netflix was my favorite.

I watched so many series. I had never seen Bull before. I watched all the seasons. After watching about 15 episodes, there was an episode that showed a woman with endometrial cancer (well what do you know)?! The lady in the episode had a husband and 2 small children and her diagnosis was terminal: she was given only 2 years to live. I boldly watched the entire show and still trusted God for me and my upcoming report.

My 2-week check-up was slowly approaching (scheduled for February 21, 2024). I would learn at this appointment what stage my cancer is, and if I needed chemo or radiation therapy and whether it had spread outside of my uterus. I prepared my questions for the doctor days in advance:

1. What are the limitations to what I can do physically?

2. Will Dr. Caiseda still be my GYN?

3. Will I always be seen by you as an oncologist now that cancer has entered my body?

4. I have discomfort in my lower abdomen, is that normal?

5. How long will I need to use a stool softener?

While headed to my 1st post-op appointment with the oncologist, I made sure I was dressed nicely because my husband and son had been seeing me in pajamas for 6 weeks now (in other words, I was looking a mess). My son drove me and the hubby. He played his gospel playlist the whole ride there (about a 25-minute ride). Jekalyn Carr's song "You Will Win" came on. Of course, I was praising God and then, Something About That Name Jesus by Rance Allen came on and we just praised God even more. I walked in the Dr's Office with my son and hubby on each side of me. They both looked nervous but were trying to hold it together for me. I had never seen that look in them before. As I went up to the check-in counter, they both stood next to me as if they were protecting me and I said, "I am okay, guys. You can sit down." I had never seen each of them so focused on me like that before. The intake technician immediately said, "Oh my, they love you" and then she said, "What a blessing to have 2 bodyguards." I smiled and said: "Indeed it is."

They called my name, and I told Tony (my hubby) to come with me while AJ (my sonshine) remained in the waiting area. Dr. Gamble came in and greeted us with a smile and a hello and asked how I was feeling. I told her I had some questions for her. She let me ask my questions and then she read her report. She proceeded to say the cancer is a grade 1 and a stage 1. It was contained within the uterus, and we were able to remove it all. There was a small tumor, and we did send it for testing and will discuss that a little further after your next follow-up. You will not need any type of therapy; however, you will be under my care for the next 5 years to get scans done every 4 to 6 months. She then said (with a big smile) this was the best we could hope for. I just kept saying thank you Jesus and the hubby kept saying "I told you; I knew you were going to be okay!"

There is an emotional and physical exhaustion that I felt for 2 additional days, even after the good report. There are so many more things that you must think about now concerning your health...things that you never had to consider before. As you begin healing from the inside out, don't rush it. Respect the healing process and stay in rest mode. Don't try to immerse yourself back into the swing of things. Trust me, it will come soon enough. Take small steps back towards your new normal, hectic life both physically and mentally. Take breaks from people when necessary. People will not stop "peopling" and life will not stop "lifeing!" Do not allow them to dump their burdens on you while you are dealing with your own issues of life. People can really be inconsiderate at your most delicate state.

The road to full recovery is steady. Continue to prepare your questions for each appointment. My 6 weeks check-up was March 22, 2024. The questions I had were:

1. My mobility has been very minimal for fear of causing damage to my insides. Is it possible to be referred to an occupational therapist due to my arthritis in my knees and back?

2. I see my primary care doctor next week via telehealth. Should I see her in person to get blood and urine drawn?

3. Can you give me a referral to a dietician to help get this weight gain under control?

4. I am in the process of writing a book regarding my cancer journey. It's a book that will have a few other cancer survivor stories in it. I am the lead visionary and 10% of the proceeds from sales will go to cancer research. Would you be willing to write the foreword or a short hopeful and supporting paragraph? I will let you read the draft before you make your decision.

Right after my doctor's visit, I had a vision of the front cover of the book. The front cover would show someone knocking on the door holding a wrapped gift to give to the person that opens the door. Also, the depiction of the background would depict some type of whirlwind, but after the catastrophe things are settled.

If this was a sermon, I would have the praise team sing "What a Beautiful Name" by Hillsong Worship. My God!

Stay Strong (FIGHT. PRAY. SLAY.)

I must say that I have had the most supportive, loving, caring, helpful, sensitive, understanding (most times), and wonderful husband a woman could ask for. This journey is not for the weary. My husband waited on me hand and foot, bathed me (the one time I let him), prayed for me, cooked for me, served me, loved me and protected me to the best of his ability. I am so very grateful. I have seen women and men go through illnesses with their spouses and they were abandoned because the healthy spouse did not want to take care of them. He is truly my best friend, indeed!

Well after 6 weeks of this major surgery, you are only halfway healed. You are feeling better, but the inside is still healing, mending and repositioning in its new form. So here is a funny story:

Hubby: *feeling on me and trying to kiss me and caress me*

Me: *Babe, I'm not healthy enough for this.*

Hubby: *Okay.*

Me: *Babe, after my healing time I promise you, it will be worth the wait!*

Hubby: *complete silence*

Me: *Why you not saying anything?*

Hubby: *What am I supposed to say?!*

Me: *Say something!*

Hubby: *I will be dead and gone!*

Me: *laughing uncontrollably for days, using all my stomach muscles*

Hubby: *complete silence*

A book and the author that I referenced during this journey was "Power Moves" by Sarah Jakes Roberts. The book spoke about the power that God gives you to complete the assignment given to you. The author says in the book that "God doesn't just understand the assignment. God understands who is holding the assignment, too. You can expect that strength, wisdom, creativity, courage and connection will meet you every step of your yes."

When I tell you, this here was the most challenging thing, I have ever had to go through in my life, but I did not feel consumed because I knew God would be with me regardless of the outcome. There is nothing too hard for God. I will always vow to say yes to the Lord, because when I have said no to him, it always turned out bad for me. I encourage you to move with power, move with authority and move with intentionality. When you think about a soldier, you think about endurance, bravery, battle, boldness, leadership, loneliness, etc. As a soldier in the army of the Lord, you will face many things, but you will have all the resources you need to fight! **When cancer knocks at your door, fight, pray and slay the giant!**

By now you realize that music is an important part of my life. I was born loving it and I will die loving it. Let me give you this one song that dropped in my spirit:

I Am Changing by Jennifer Holiday

Listen! Look at me! I am changing. Wow I have heard this song over 30 years so many times and have even seen Jennifer Holiday perform it in person when I was a teenager, but HONEY, this thing hits different now! When you have a face to face with death and God allows you to live, HONTEE! You gonna change! You better change! Everything around you is gonna change because a shift is supposed to occur. So, get ready for family and friends to look at you funny. Get prepared to be misunderstood because the vision given to you is not for them to understand. Just ask God for strength

and put those shades on and focus on the prize (your purpose, goals and dreams). The rest God will take care of.

As I move forward and under the oncologist's care, I do not pretend to be emotionless and unafraid. I experience anxieties every time I feel a new or awkward pain in my body. I get emotional every time I visit the doctor or get a scan. I get nervous and anxious sometimes when I think about the unknown, but I press on because I have witnessed too many victories to have defeat have the last word. I have seen too many soldiers **FIGHT, PRAY, AND SLAY the giant!**

Resources

Books:

5-year Diary

The Garden within by Dr. Anita Phillips

Destined to Win by Tammy Vaughn (Co-Author Rhonda Hatton)

Do it Afraid by Joyce Meyer

The Hill We Climb by Amanda Gorman

Stores:

Amazon, Dollar Tree, Dollar General, Ross, Massage Envy

Therapists:

EAP, Primary Doctor and Oncologist will give you a referral

Hospitals:

MedStar

Insurance: Aetna PPO, Life Insurance (some policies have early withdrawal addendums)

About the Author

LaDonna Stanley-Thompson

I am LaDonna Stanley-Thompson, affectionately known as Dondon by close family and friends. This sentimental name was given to me by my oldest niece (Andrea) when she was 1 year old, she is now 40+. Okay back to me! I was born in Southeast Washington, DC and grew up in the Barry Farms Dwellings. LOL, y'all like the way I make that sound like a gated suburb community huh! Well, that is how it felt being raised by my single mother, me the youngest, and my 4 older siblings Brian, Vincent, Deneane and Gary. It was my home, and I am a product (not a statistic) of this community and very proud of it. Also, I have an older half-sister (Barbara) that we met for the first time when I was 12, she has been the best big sister ever!

I am married to my childhood next-door neighbor, Mr. Anthony Thompson, Sr., whom I am very much still in love with. We have one son, Anthony Thompson, Jr., AKA AJ. He is our pride and joy.

I graduated from Ballou High School in 1987, then attended Morgan State University where I majored in Elementary Education. I transferred to the University of the District of Columbia in 1990-1992, and I am currently a student at Columbia Southern University majoring in Organizational Management. I am also a proud Federal Government Employee of 25 years. Additionally, I am the Co-Founder and Executive Director of my family's Non-Profit Organization that was started in 2013 in memory of my beautiful mother, the late Martha Stanley. The Stanley House of LOVE (SHoLOVE) is an organization that gives back to the community through scholarships, mentorship, community service, honoring public servants annually, and a host of other community ventures.

I enjoy the little things in life, like spending time with family and friends, going to church to worship and to fellowship with my sisters and Brothers in Christ, traveling, dreaming, and believing that anything is possible. Yep, I don't ask for much!

Finally, I am a first-time author and a first-time cancer survivor. My God is so good!

Part 2:

Three Battles, One Warrior

by Desiree Waters

Three Battles, One Warrior

Desiree Waters

When I was five years old, I could not have imagined how my life would turn out. My path was unknown, but I remember thoughts of being married, having kids, and making lots of money. All of which were typical fantasies for a kid back then.

At fourteen I dedicated my life to the Lord, not realizing how that decision would eventually shape my life and revolutionize my thinking. The evolution of this relationship became my guiding force and strength.

During my junior year of high school, I had the privilege of participating in a program called Work Study. This program provided high school students with good grades with the opportunity to work part-time while continuing their high school education. For several hours, a day I worked in the Baltimore City Police Department. This is where I acquired my enthusiasm for the business world. It was this experience that matured me, changed my focus, opened doors of opportunities that helped me achieve many of my dreams, goals, and aspirations.

In 1998 I married for a second time, to a wonderful man of God. We blended our families and started a ministry together. Life was sweet with a few hiccups along the way. However, throughout most of my life, I never gave any thought to the "what if's" from a health perspective. I always took care of my body by getting regular checkups, mammograms, etc.

In 2010 my father became ill. His health started to decline, and my stepmother needed assistance, and I was in a place that I could help. Although I lived 45 minutes away, that did not matter because I would do anything for them. I was with him 4 days a week and as his health continued to decline, five days a week. It was during this time that I stopped taking care of myself.

In the year leading up to my dad's death, I was having pain in my right breast and in my spirit, I knew something was wrong, but I kept putting everything and everybody before me. In 2017 my dad passed. A few months later I made a mammogram appointment. Throughout that appointment, a feeling kept coming over me "somethings wrong." After the mammogram, I sat in the waiting room, awaiting my results. The nurse finally told me that I needed a second mammogram. Shortly after, I received a call from Kaiser to schedule a digital mammogram. Once the doctor reviewed both mammograms, he recommended an ultrasound guided biopsy because he found a small suspicious mass in my right breast. The biopsy results were positive for cancer. I was Instantly referred to the Multidisciplinary Breast Cancer Clinic at Kaiser.

When I first heard the word cancer, I automatically associated it with death, like many others. I was saddened by the news but not surprised.

After my diagnosis, Kaiser contacted me to discuss my next steps. The first step was to meet my designated Cancer Team. This team consisted of an oncologist, radiation oncologist, surgeon, and nurse. I remember my husband and I having to meet with one right after another, each one gave their perspective based on their field and presented us with additional information. My head was spinning! It was clear that the decision had already been made, that I needed a lumpectomy. In that moment, I felt as if I was being rushed to decide. It is as if I did not have enough time to think things over because my life was ticking away.

On the way home, neither of us said much of anything. We were trying to process everything we were told. Over the next several days, I just cried. Every time I thought about the diagnosis the tears would flow. I decided right away not to share my diagnosis with anyone until I could fully come to grips with it and was up to answering questions.

After days of crying and praying, I finally shook myself, regained my composure and started reading the pamphlets provided and doing my own research. I have always been an investigator at heart. And I uncovered a lot of information that would prove to be beneficial. **You can find more about What is Cancer & Recommended Resources on pages 61-63.**

One week before my lumpectomy, I told my family and friends. Everyone was supportive. However, a family member told me that they felt as if my immediate family should have been a part of my decision-making process. I remember saying to myself, "No one has the right unless asked to weigh-in on my life or deaf decision." My husband said, "this decision should only be made by you, for you." And I agreed!

On November 7, 2017, I had a Lumpectomy and a sentinel lymph node biopsy. A lymph node is a small bean shaped organ which produces and stores blood cells that help fight disease and infection.

The day of surgery they placed a breast lesion site marker in my breast. This marker indicated to the surgeon exactly where my mass was. They also gave me a needle in my nipple. **This needle had a radioactive tracer dye in it that travels to the lymph nodes under the armpit to let the surgeon know which ones to remove. Before giving me the needle, the nurse** said, "you're going to feel this, but I'm going to spray some icy on your nipple to help numb it." When she put that needle in my nipple, I have never, In my life, even after experiencing labor pains for 37 hours, felt that kind of pain. The pain was so horrific that I had an outer body experience. Believe me when I say, after that needle, I was not in my right mind, I could not speak or process information.

The surgery was a success; but I tested positive for cancer in my lymph nodes. Which meant, I had stage 2 breast cancer. Stage 2 is when the tumor is 2 to 5 centimeters and the cancer spreads to the lymph nodes.

While I was recuperating, I was blessed to have all my loved one's rally around. But it was my husband that had everything under control. He cooked, cleaned, and loved on me. He was by my side every step of the way! However, I was not oblivious as to how this ordeal affected him. I knew he was overly concerned and cried over the situation. Both of us were uncertain how our life would be after cancer.

A few weeks after the surgery I met with my oncologist. During the meeting I was educated on my next course of action, based on the surgery and tissue samples taken during surgery. My oncologist recommended radiation treatments and the 5-year pill (Anastrozole). All of which I declined because I wanted to take a holistic approach.

Once I told him this, his hands were tied. You see, the insurance companies have a path that they want all doctors and patients to follow based on research and studies. In this case, it was the American Cancer Society. In addition to that, their computer system blocks them from selecting any treatment outside of the predesignated ones. This includes doctor referrals, treatments, and services. They want everybody to follow the same path. Yet, as much as my oncologist could, he helped with my holistic journey. Although he did not agree with my choice, he respected it.

To my surprise, the oncology department automatically enrolled me in a program that provided financial aid. The program is called Kaiser Permanente Medical Financial Assistance. This was truly a blessing. This program eliminated my prescription and co-pay cost for the first 5 years. If you know anything about cancer, it can be very costly. **You can find more information on pages 64-71.**

My Holistic Journey

To begin my holistic journey, I met with an alternative doctor. An alternative doctor deals with your diet, exercise, sleep, rest, and emotional wellbeing. She was great! The first thing she did was to find out my blood type, which enabled her to map out a diet and exercise plan especially for me. **You can find more** *information on pages 72-84. Stores, Food & Recipes pages 85-87, Health Markers & Holistic Support pages 88-91.*

My New Life

Because of my lifestyle changes, I lost 35 pounds by simply changing the way I ate with moderate exercise. I also did a cleanse, using The Master Cleanser by Stanley Burroughs as my guide for 30 days. Over the next 3 years I stuck to this regiment.

Just before the world shut down due to COVID-19 in March of 2020. I suffered a head injury. This is when I began eating unhealthy foods because all I could do was sit around. I regained the 35 pounds I originally lost. After getting through that hurdle, I started to regain some sense of normality in my life again, however I started having pain in my right breast. I had been getting mammograms every six months and nothing was showing up. I kept telling my primary care physician and oncologist that I was experiencing pain in my right breast, and everybody kept saying but your mammograms are normal. Again, I felt as if "something was wrong."

Note: Some doctors say that cancer has no pain associated with it. However, there are several individuals that I know personally that experienced pain in their breasts prior to being diagnosed. Everyone's journey and experiences are different, and cancer is not one size fits all.

On April 5, 2023, I had an x-ray mammogram and like before, I had to go back for a digital mammogram. The second one showed a new mass, so I had another biopsy on May 11th, and I tested positive for breast cancer in my right breast for a second time. I had just passed my five-year milestone in November of 2022.

Cancer survivors mark the five-year anniversary of their diagnosis as a benchmark for when they can say that their chances of having the cancer return are no longer likely. This is because some doctors may say that someone is cured if they remain in complete remission for five years or more. Complete remission means that all symptoms and signs of cancer go away, and there is no detectable cancer in the body. However, some cancer cells can remain in your body for many years after treatment, and these cells may cause the cancer to come back.

Like before, I was asked to meet with my cancer team which consisted of the same oncologist, but everyone else was new. When I met with my new surgeon, I requested that she remove my right breast. She refused, she said, "that is not necessary, and I do not recommend it." In my mind, it was a clever idea because I was eliminating the possibility of a recurrence of cancer a third time.

Going through this process for a second time, I immediately noticed some of Kaiser's procedures had changed. This time around, they placed the breast lesion site marker in several days before surgery.

On July 26, 2023, the day of surgery, they put that needle in my nipple. Unlike before, I knew what to expect, so I requested extra numbing cream and a pain pill. Even after my attempts to decrease the pain, it was still horrific!

The surgery was successful and to my surprise my lymph nodes tested negative for cancer. This time around I was classified as a stage one cancer patient.

During my first visit to my oncologist after the surgery, he said the tissue sample, taken during surgery yielded the same results. Meaning, I developed the same type of cancer for a second time. He recommended, or should I say, pleaded with me to complete radiation treatments and take the five-year pill. It was as if he was implying that I got cancer a second time because I refused radiation treatments and the pill, the first time. I did not feel that way and I will explain why.

My childhood friend was diagnosed with breast cancer in 2016, the year before my first diagnosis. She elected to undergo radiation treatments and take the five-year pill. She did not experience any side effects. However, she was diagnosed with breast cancer for a second time in 2023 in the same breast and they told her that the five-year pill had just stopped working. It is these types of stories why I do not believe they fully understand why cancer is recurring.

I elected the second time to take my oncologist and my husband's advice and undergo radiation treatments 5 days a week for 6 weeks and take the five-year pill.

Kaiser did not have any radiation locations close to my residence, so they referred me to an outside clinic. However, they failed to communicate it would cost $45 per visit, which is a total of $1,350. After finding that out, I decided to go to a Kaiser location where I did not have a copay. When I let the offsite office manager know, she told me that there is a percentage of funds that a doctor can write off each year. She asked me to give her a few days to speak to the radiation doctors. To my surprise, I was told that they decided to wave my copay. Always remember to let your doctor know if you have any financial issues or just cannot afford to add this cost to your existing budget.

My radiation treatments were challenging to say the least. I was burnt severely on my breast, neck, underarm and shoulder. To the point where they had to prescribe Silver Sulfadiazine Cream, a burn cream. My breast had the texture of alligator skin and although that is gone, my skin is still dark and burnt looking in those areas. Radiation also tapped into my energy levels. There were days where I could barely make it home. If I were out running errands, whenever I started feeling fatigued, I could not press pass it. I had to stop whatever I was doing and get to a place where I could sit or lay down. As of 2024, I am still dealing with the lack of energy. I have been told by people with similar experiences that they did not regain their energy until a year after radiation.

The five-year pill (ANASTROZOLE) my oncologist prescribed gave me hot flashes every 15 minutes. I could not endure that because I had hot flashes for about 15 years straight when I started menopause. That was enough to last me a lifetime. I asked for something different, and he prescribed (EXEMESTANE) and this has been working. I still get flashes periodically, so my doctor prescribed CITALOPRAM and I love it. Where was this medication 30 years ago? Always remember, if something is not working for you, usually your doctor can prescribe something different.

Throughout both journeys, I was blessed to have great and supportive doctors. It has always been imperative that I form a relationship with every doctor and that we listen to each other, because I know my body best of all.

My Mental Health

Never having to experience mental health issues, I could not imagine the toll this second diagnosis would take on my mental health. I cannot explain when or how I got to this depleted place. I just started to feel as if life had been sucked out of me. I could not pray, I sat around in a daze, I did not want to live. I felt as if I could not get a break from dealing with health issues. I went to a place mentally that I knew not of. I would tell people how I felt. Some did not know what to say, some said "I'll be praying for you," while others began to pray, immediately.

One evening, my brother and sister-in-love called to check on me. I remember crying on the phone, which is extremely unusual for me. I do not remember what I said, but after that call, they knew I needed them to come see about me. In my heart, I knew I needed them to survive, and I was not going to make it without physically having them around. My brother has a large family, and I have always admired their bond and when my brother put the word out, they responded. And just like that, I was surrounded by an abundance of love! If I had not been surrounded by family, friends, and godchildren I am not sure where I would be mentally. There were many things that helped draw me out of that dark place. It was my incredible family, friends and godchildren, prayers, calls, text messages, visits, meals, flowers, gifts, and the overwhelming feeling of being loved and supported.

In our community we tend to not tell people how we really feel but I was not shy about telling anyone how I felt. As I am typing, tears are flowing, because there is no verbiage to describe where I was mentally. All I can say is, it was a very dark place that I never want to visit again!

OH NO, NOT AGAIN!

My Third Cancer Diagnosis

During the process of drafting my story, and just one radiation treatment away from finishing my second bout with breast cancer, on October 28, 2023, I was sitting on the side of my bed when the left side of my face went numb. It felt like I had been given Novocaine.

Immediately, I contacted my oncologist and radiation oncologist to ask if the radiation treatments could be the cause. Both said there was no connection, but I was referred to a neurologist. After I explained my symptoms, he replied, "Maybe the numbness is related to the treatment, and if so, I suppose at this point there is not much to do other than put up with it." I replied, "Put up with my face being numb? I told him quickly, I refused to accept that. He immediately referred me to a neurosurgeon at the Washington Brain & Spine Institute. After meeting with the doctor, he ordered a PET scan, MRI, and lumbar puncture. On March 14, 2024, I was informed by my neurosurgeon that the test showed an abnormality on the left side of my head behind my left eye, which they called an angioma. He assured me it was nothing, but because of my cancer history, he wanted a biopsy. He had already concluded that the angioma was inoperable because it was attached to my nervous system; removing it would leave me blind and cause permanent facial numbness.

The neurosurgeon decided not to access the angioma through my head. The best approach was through my nose, requiring the expertise of an otolaryngologist (Ear, Nose, and Throat Surgeon). On July 16, 2024, I had an endoscopic image-guided transsphenoidal biopsy of the sphenoid bone and was hospitalized for four days. After surgery, both surgeons said they were confident the specimen did not look cancerous. However, the results were pending. Just before discharge, I learned that my biopsy results would be sent to Johns Hopkins Medical Center for a second opinion. A wave of unease washed over me, but I trusted both surgeons and tried to dismiss my worries.

When I got home, I was in constant pain. I had a follow-up appointment on July 22nd with my surgeon. I asked her how long before the pain subsided. She said, "You'll start to feel better around August 19th." I replied, August 19th? That is 28 days away. She explained the severity of my surgery, saying that although I had no visible facial scarring, accessing the skull is extremely painful.

Remember the horrific pain I described from the needle in my nipple? I was wrong. This pain was debilitating and constant.

For the next four weeks, I experienced nasal and throat bleeding, throbbing headaches, vomiting, stabbing head pain, and foreign-looking packing discharging from my nose. Had the doctor not warned me, I would have thought pieces of my skull were coming out.

On August 14th, I received a call from my surgeon. My biopsy results were in, and they were positive for cancer. The biopsy consisted of bone fragments with surrounding dense fibrosis. There was a focal irregular proliferation of nests and tubules of epithelial cells with a moderate amount of eosinophilic cytoplasm and large, hyperchromatic, irregular nuclei. In short, I was diagnosed with metastatic breast cancer that had spread to the sphenoid bone in my skull. I later learned that there was an actual hole in my skull bone.

Both surgeons were shocked by the results and apologized for what they had told me in the hospital. I was not surprised at all.

Because the cancer was in my skull bone, and the lesion was behind my left eye, my oncologist wanted treatment to begin immediately. He referred me to a radiation center specializing in head treatments.

I learned that radiation to the head is different than to the breast, and that, miraculously, the hole in my skull bone would mend itself. After my consultation, the radiation oncologist recommended five days of 15-minute treatments. The first step was creating a full head mask to ensure my head remained perfectly still during treatment. I was told not to change my hairstyle because any change would affect how the mask would fit. On September 13, 2024, I began radiation treatments. The first day of treatment when they locked my head into that tight mask, I felt claustrophobic. I lay on that table with tears rolling down my face. ***View the mask below:***

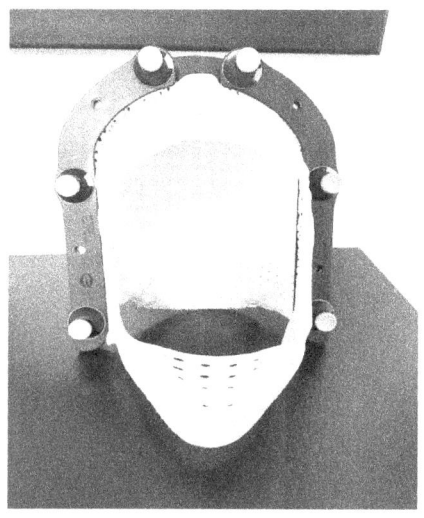

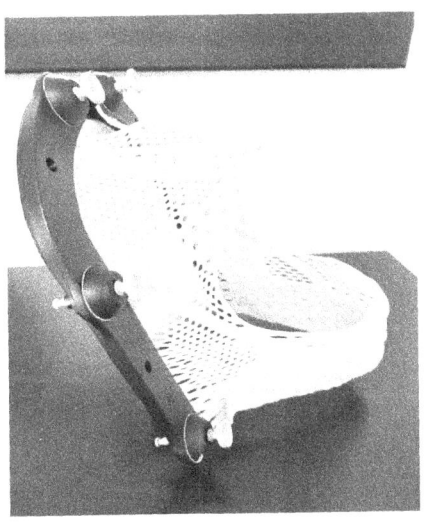

During the treatments, I experienced loss of taste, stabbing head pain, nausea, and facial and finger numbness. After the treatments, I began taking medication. Because this was my third bout with cancer, my oncologist prescribed medication typically used for stage 4 cancer patients.

I struggled with the side effects of the medication:

- Kisqali: This medication has numerous side effects, including lung, liver, and heart rhythm problems, severe skin reactions, loss of taste and low white blood cell count. These are just a few of the extensive lists of potential side effects. While taking Kisqali, bi-weekly blood tests and periodic EKGs are required.

- Letrozole: Side effects include headache, loss of appetite, metallic taste, skin rash, sleepiness, hot flashes, dizziness, fast heartbeat, nausea, and joint pain.

The severity of these medications became clear when I was assigned a personal Oncology Clinical Pharmacy Specialist. She monitors all my prescribed medications to ensure there are no negative interactions and reviews all labs and test results to protect my health.

A few weeks after treatment, I began experiencing moderate hearing loss in my left ear. I saw an Audiologist who conducted an audiogram. The test showed that I had in fact had some hearing loss. The doctor explained that it is common to experience hearing loss when undergoing radiation treatments and your over age 65. I was also prescribed 4mg of dexamethasone to decrease any inflammation in my ear that could also be contributing to my loss of hearing.

This book will be published before my next MRI and PET scan, which will inform my oncologists whether the radiation treatments were successful or if I require additional treatments.

My journey is far from over. However, I know for sure that I will fight with everything I have. And I will continue to ask God for the strength to take it one day at a time.

In closing, I encourage anyone starting their cancer journey to follow their instincts. Do what is best for you. What works for one person may not work for another. Surround yourself with supportive people who encourage you and speak life into you, and fight with everything you have.

To the family and friends of cancer patients: We understand that life is busy, but remember, we make time for what is important to us.

When someone is in need or sick, it rarely fits into our schedules, but that is when we choose what matters most.

Calls are appreciated, but a visit can lift our spirits in ways that a call cannot.

My great-nephew came to visit one night, and I later learned that he had canceled something that was especially important to him, just to see about me. He told me how important I was to him. I was deeply touched, and it brought tears to my eyes. This is a perfect example of the kind of love and support I am talking about.

This journey can feel lonely and loveless at times, especially after a third bout with cancer. There was a time when I struggled with my family showing me love. I know they love me, but I needed the action of love, not the word. I remember my husband giving me a word from the Lord. He said, "The Lord wants you to receive love from where He sends it. Stop looking for love from people you are wanting to love you in the way you want to be loved."

One thing is for sure, when I am gone, I cannot see or feel any acts of love. So please, give me my flowers while I can smell them and show me the action of love not just the word.

Desiree Waters

Information & Resources

First Things First: *What is Cancer?*

Pharmaceutical Research Journal: "Cancer is a preventable disease that requires major lifestyle changes."

Cancer is a malignant tumor that forms in the body. (Dead cells replicating themselves throughout your body) However, tumors form in the body **to** save your life.

1. Tumors form because the body is trying to fight off infection. So, the tumor houses the toxins.
2. These tumors use carbohydrates and sugars to generate energy. The rapid growth of these cells is associated with cellular metabolism.
3. Cancer cannot exist in an oxygen rich and alkaline environment/body.
4. Cancer cells need an acidic environment as this will enable them to grow and spread at a higher rate.
5. 5.5% of cancer comes from genetics/DNA (Time Magazine) not your destiny.
6. Sugar feeds cancer cells.
7. According to a study done by the Department of Radiology in Sydney, 2.1% of cancer patients benefit from chemotherapy.
8. Radiation and chemotherapy increase circulating tumor cells and stem cells. The Stanford School of

Medicine found that shrinking a cancer tumor may offer temporary relief but will not offer a long-term cure if the cancer stem cells are not illuminated. Stem cells (found in embryos or adults) are responsible for migration and metastasis.

9. Chemotherapy was originally based on mustard gas from World War 1 & 2.

10. Radiation burns away healthy tissue.

11. No one knows how many tumors cells are circulating in your body.

12. Stress is a large part of any illness.

Recommended Resources:

Book: The Only Answer to Cancer by Dr. Leonard Coldwell

Support Groups:

1. Hope Connections for Cancer Support, they offer free, professionally led programs for people with cancer and their loved ones dealing with the emotional and physical impact of cancer.

    (https://hopeconnectionsforcancer.org/)

2. A free program for newly diagnosed breast cancer patients called Breast Cancer Buddies. They hold monthly zoom meetings to share resources.

    (http://www.expressivetherapycenter.com/breast-cancer-buddies)

HealthCentral

What's the Average Cost of Breast Cancer Treatment?

Breast cancer treatment is both essential and expensive—but there are ways to lessen the financial burden.

May 17, 2023
By:

Breast cancer the is expensive to treat. Reasons include sophisticated new treatments that offer more personalized care for specific breast cancer types, as well as costly diagnostic and disease management tools like pathology and lab tests. Depending on your breast cancer stage, type, and medication needs, your cost of treatment can vary widely. The most recent figures indicate the of for one patient could range from $20,000 to $100,000.

It's a —especially with having less than $500 in savings. Let's look deeper into these numbers—and what you can do about mitigating the high cost of breast cancer treatment.

Cost

Cost of Breast Cancer Care

Cancer in general is costly. National expenditures for all cancer types totaled $208.9 billion in 2020, the most recent date for federal statistics according to the National Cancer Institute (NCI). Female breast cancer is the most expensive type of cancer, with national expenditures estimated at $29.8 billion in 2020, the NCI reports. A 2021 study in *JAMA Network Open* found that patients with breast cancer had the most services performed (especially for pathology and laboratory tests) and incurred the highest costs than other forms of the disease, particularly for medical supplies and nonphysician services.

Breast cancer treatment costs also vary based on subtype of breast cancer and the stage at diagnosis, says Susan Brown, R.N., the senior director of health information and publications at Susan G. Komen in Dallas, TX. Treatment type costs vary, too, from one-time surgery to targeted therapy that can last up to a year to hormonal/endocrine therapy that can last for up to 10 years.

Insurance vs. Out of Pocket

Health Insurance Costs vs. Out-of-Pocket Expenses

Depending on your health insurance, many, but not all, costs associated with breast cancer treatment may be covered—but not everyone has insurance or the same level of insurance coverage. "There are extreme variations in cost, not only related to the treatment necessary, but also related to who is paying for the treatment," Brown explains. For instance, if insurance companies are paying for care, they negotiate prices with providers, she says, so the cost may be less than someone who is paying out-of-pocket.

"Also, each insurance policy is different—with different co-pays, coverage, and lifetime limits—so the actual out-of-pocket cost varies," Brown says. "At the end of the day, it is the health insurers who set the prices and determine how much patients have to pay out-of-pocket."

And the cost of breast cancer treatment isn't measured just in health insurance premiums (how much you pay monthly for your health insurance policy), your deductible (the amount you pay for out-of-pocket costs before the plan pays), co-pays, and related costs you can see on an

Desiree Waters

Sign up for our monthly Breast Cancer Newsletter.

Cost by Stage

Cost of Breast Cancer Treatment by Stage

When looking at breast cancer stages (measured as 0 to 4, from least advanced to most) and the likely cost of treatment at each stage, one published retrospective analysis of 8,360 women with breast cancer found that treatment costs were higher for patients with advanced disease at diagnosis. So an earlier diagnosis could mean a lowered financial impact. Costs also decreased after the first year of treatment, but were still considered high.

The average cost of care for all stages was $85,772 for the first year after diagnosis. Broken down specifically by stage, the average cost breast cancer treatment in the first year were:

- Stage 0: $60,637
- Stage 1 and 2: $82,121
- Stage 3: $129,387
- Stage 4: $134,682

These totals reflect the procedures and treatments needed at each stage, which might include a potential lumpectomy, mastectomy, sentinel lymph node biopsy, genetic testing, chemotherapy, radiation, hormone therapy pills, immunotherapy and more, per an illustrative case study from the American Cancer Society.

Keep in mind, these totals do not account for any hidden out-of-pocket costs of care, just what's billable to your insurance company.

Direct Costs

Direct Medical Costs of Breast Cancer Treatment

So just how much does each specific breast cancer treatment cost? Take, for instance, the cost of a mastectomy or lumpectomy. Most women with early-stage breast cancer have some type of surgery, according to the American Cancer Society. With insurance, you are typically covered for the procedure itself but will pay any related co-pays, deductibles, and co-insurance out-of-pocket.

Desiree Waters

But if you don't have health insurance? A ⬚⬚⬚⬚ could cost you $15,000-$55,000, and a ⬚⬚⬚⬚ could be between $10,000-$20,000, depending on factors including where you have the surgery performed. ⬚⬚⬚⬚ are also often combined with radiation, which can add about $7,000 for whole breast radiation and around $15,000 for intensity-modulated radiation therapy to your bill.

Systemic therapies like hormonal therapy, targeted therapy, and/or chemotherapy are often used to treat more advanced cancers. These treatments can run into the thousands of dollars. Newer treatments are targeted in their approach. The medication ⬚⬚⬚⬚ ⬚⬚⬚⬚, for example, just treats women with metastatic HER2-negative breast cancer with an inherited BRCA1 or BRCA2 mutation who have received chemotherapy before—but can come with a hefty price tag, retailing at an average of more than ⬚⬚⬚⬚.

Older drugs often used in combination with newer treatments can also be expensive. ⬚⬚⬚⬚ can cost up to $48,000 a year for four treatments. ⬚⬚⬚⬚, which can be taken years after initial breast cancer treatment, can cost $10 to $85 per month.

Still, these costs are all averages. "It is difficult to give specifics about the costs of treatment to women with breast cancer because patients come to us with different insurance plans, deductibles, and co-payments," says oncologist ⬚⬚⬚⬚ ⬚⬚⬚⬚, section chief of breast surgical oncology at Smilow Cancer Hospital and Yale Cancer Center and an associate professor of surgery (oncology, breast) at Yale School of Medicine in New Haven, CT.

"As oncologists, we prioritize patient survival and quality of life above all else," Dr. Greenup adds. "Yet, it is important for us to recognize that unaffordable care makes cancer treatment difficult for patients to receive. When deciding on treatment options for our patients, we take a holistic view of women's diagnosis, values, and needs—the financial and employment impacts are important to consider."

Cost for reconstruction after breast cancer surgery can also be high. Dr. Greenup and colleagues examined the financial impact on the surgical choices of 607 women with stage 0 to III breast cancer in a ⬚⬚⬚⬚. They found that 28% of patients reported that costs of treatment influenced their surgical decisions—and at incomes of $45,000 per year "costs were prioritized over breast preservation or appearance."

⬚⬚⬚⬚

Indirect Costs of Breast Cancer Treatment

Desiree Waters

For Jessica Moorhead, 36, of Philadelphia, the financial toll of having breast cancer was as much about indirect, as direct, costs. Diagnosed at age 32 with early-stage triple negative breast cancer, she's since progressed to metastatic disease. "For me, the biggest financial impact is that I've had to stop working due to breast cancer," Moorhead says. "Especially because I was so young, it took me out of my working years at my peak-earning capacity."

Indeed, research has found that wage loss is an important financial consequence of breast cancer. Other indirect costs for Moorhead include trialing medications until she found an effective one—all while paying drug co-pays for meds she's likely to never take again. She's had to purchase over-the-counter vitamins to help with fatigue. She's had to invest in new clothes following surgery and lymphedema.

"They're just more out-of-pocket kinds of things to try to address, not necessarily the actual cancer, but all the side effects and problems that it's caused," she says. "I would say the lifestyle modifications and things that I feel like I have to keep buying to make myself comfortable as my body changes are some of the hidden costs of it."

Other indirect costs for breast cancer patients can include:

- **Acupuncture.** Often used as complementary care for pain, nausea and vomiting, and lymphedema in breast cancer treatment, acupuncture can cost over $100 on average for a first visit, then $80 for follow-up sessions. Some insurance plans will cover acupuncture; others don't.
- **Childcare.** You may need someone to watch your child during and after breast cancer treatments. A nanny can cost almost $700 a week for one child and a child care center can cost more than $220 per week for one child, according to Care.com.
- **Mental health therapy.** Therapy can help you get through the emotional highs and lows of the cancer experience, but it can range from $65 per hour to $250 per hour for in-person sessions. Health insurance will often have mental health coverage, so check in with your plan.
- **New diet.** You might want to change how you eat to include more fruits and vegetables, which research shows may benefit women diagnosed with breast cancer. But with all food prices set to increase 6.5% in 2023, eating more fresh foods can be costly.
- **Physical therapy (PT).** Having PT might be necessary to help with pain and mobility issues after surgery. When you're insured and have met your deductible, average out-

Desiree Waters

of-pocket cost can be between $20 to 900. If you're uninsured, it can cost $30 to $155.

Scalp cooling systems/cold caps. These are used to help prevent hair loss from chemo but they aren't universally covered by health insurance. Scalp cooling _____ for a full course of chemo. Cold caps can cost $380 to $450 per month plus shipping and other fees.

Wigs. After hair loss from chemotherapy, many women undergoing breast cancer treatment opt for a wig. They can _____ anywhere from $30 to thousands of dollars.

_____ Getting to and from radiation therapy alone—sometimes five days a week, up to 10 weeks—adds up. You need gas money to get to your treatment center, possibly money for parking, and the general upkeep of a car with added mileage. If you can't drive, you might need a rideshare or public transportation.

How to Save on Breast Cancer Treatment

So what, if anything, can you do to help reduce the cost of care for breast cancer treatment? Start with these expert-approved tips.

Talk With Your Doctor About Treatment Costs

Ask if your cancer treatment center or hospital system has a nurse navigator, social worker, or other health professional who can help you navigate the finances involved in breast cancer treatment. Find someone that you're comfortable talking to and share your financial concerns, suggests Jean Sachs, CEO of _____, a nonprofit based in Bala Cynwyd, PA. The breast cancer organization provides accurate information, a supportive community, and resources to ease the financial burden of medical care.

Lean on Family and Friends

When family and friends ask how they can help, have ideas that involve financial needs at the ready, Sachs recommends. Instead of yet another frozen casserole or lasagna, say what you really you need is someone to sort through medical bills or pick your kids up from school.

Desiree Waters

Ask for Drug Discounts

Pharmaceutical companies will often offer patient assistance programs (PAPs) to help people afford medications, according to the Centers for Medicare & Medicaid Services. They can help with financial assistance or other help. For instance, the company that makes Lynparza, AstraZeneca, offers a $0 co-pay for all eligible patients, as well as the AstraZeneca Access 360™ program, which helps "streamline access and reimbursement" for the med. Check if your medication has a PAP.

Tap Into Patient Advocacy Networks

Accessing the right resources can give you a head start on handling breast cancer treatment costs. The organizations here are a good place to start:

- Hair to Stay Foundation and Sharsheret: Both provide need-based grants to pay for some scalp cooling costs.
- Lazarex Cancer Foundation: The only organization in the U.S. that not only finds cancer clinical trials for patients, but also reimburses them for out-of-pocket travel costs associated with participating in a clinical trial.
- Living Beyond Breast Cancer: Has breast cancer resources, support, and financial info for patients.
- Patient Advocate Foundation: This national non-profit organization provides case management services and financial aid to Americans with chronic, life-threatening, and debilitating illnesses, including cancer.
- Susan G. Komen: The org offers a range of support services to people going through breast cancer through its Patient Care Center.
- The Rapunzel Project: The non-profit org helps people undergoing chemo have access to scalp cooling technology.
- Triage Cancer: This national non-profit organization gives free education on practical and legal issues related to a cancer diagnosis. Among other helpful material, it provides free Cancer Rights Guides to patients for learning more about insurance, finance, and the law.

Pick the Right Insurance Plan

Desiree Waters

If you don't need the insurance enrollment window, look at the premium costs, out-of-pocket costs, formularies (covered drug list), and provider networks of the plans available. Then try to pick the plan that will be by far the best match for your situation across all of these areas. [illegible] a health advocacy analyst for Healthline Network and the Susan Komen M[?], recommends.

Since you'll hit your out-of-pocket limit fairly quickly, a plan with the lowest total cost of monthly premiums and annual out-of-pocket limit might be your best option. But as in so many things, there are multiple factors to consider. If you have a higher deductible plan, you might find that your out-of-pocket costs are very high in the first month or two, and then zero out fairly quickly. If you have a low deductible plan, your costs might be spread out over a longer time frame, which might be easier to manage. [illegible] Nonz. You can also ask your doctor's or medical facilities about payment plans that might make it easier to manage your costs, even if your health plan front-loads them with a large deductible.

The Bottom Line

No matter what health insurance plan you pick, or what helps you with some of any tough financial choices you face with breast cancer treatment, the cost of breast cancer can be unusually high. "The impact of breast cancer is not only measured in sheer dollars and cents and hospital bills," Moorhead points out, "but all these other parts of the equation, of the living with it, keeping your body as well as it can be, are harder to quantify, but are still expected."

Keep working with your medical team to find ways to ease the burden of care — and know that with today's treatments, your odds of a successful outcome are greater than ever.

Desiree Waters

BLOOD TYPE B
Adapted from EAT RIGHT FOR YOUR TYPE
By DR. D'ADAMO

	BENEFICIAL	NEUTRAL	AVOID
MEAT	Lamb, rabbit, venison, goat	Beef, buffalo, liver, pheasant, veal, turkey, calf liver, mutton, ostrich,	Bacon, chicken, Cornish hens, duck, goose, grouse, guinea hen, beef heart, horse, ham, heart, pork, partridge, quail, squab, squirrel, turtle
FISH	Caviar, cod, croaker, flounder, grouper, haddock, hake, halibut, harvest fish, mackerel, mahi mahi monkfish, Ocean perch, pickerel, pike, porgy, salmon, sardine, shad, sea trout, shad, sole, sturgeon	Abalone, Blue fish, bullhead, bluefish, carp, chub, catfish, cusk, drum, grey sole, halfmoon fish, herring, mullet, muskellunge, opaleye fish, orange roughy, perch, pompano, snapper, rose fish, sail fish, scallop, scrod, scup, shark, smelt, squid, sucker, sunfish, swordfish, tuna, weakfish, whitefish, whiting	Anchovy, barracuda, beluga, bluegill, butterfish, bass, clam, conch, crab, crayfish, eel, frog, lobster, lox, mussels, octopus, oysters, Pollack, salmon roe, sea bass, shrimp, snail, striped bass, turtle, trout, yellowtail
DAIRY	Cottage cheese, farmer, feta, goat cheese & milk, kefir, mozzarella, ricotta, skim or 2% yoghurt	Everything, including chicken eggs, except AVOID list	American, blue cheeses, ice cream, string cheese, duck, goose and quail eggs.
BEANS/LEGUMES	Kidney, lima, navy, red soy beans,	Broad, cannellini, copper, fava, jicama, northern red, snap, string/green, white bean, tamarind beans	Aduke, azuki, black, garbanzo, pinto, domestic, green/red lentils, black eyed peas, mung beans and sprouts, soy cheese (tofu), tempeh
NUTS/SEEDS	walnut	Almond butter, almonds, beech, butter, brazils, chestnuts, flaxseed, hickory, litchi, macadamia, pecans, pine, english walnuts	Brazil, cashew, pistachios, filbert (hazelnut), peanut, peanut butter, poppyseed, pumpkin seed, sesame, sunflower
CEREALS/BREADS/GRAIN/PASTA	Essene and ezekial (sprouted grain bread), Millet, oat (all), puffed rice, rice bran, SPELT, wasa breads, fin crisp, millet, rice cakes Oat flour, rice flour, Essene bread, ezekial bread, millet, puffed rice, rice bran, Spelt bread or cereal,	Barley, Famlia, farina, granola, grape nuts, quinoa, white or brown rice, Glutenfree, no wheat spelt, ideal flat & pumpernickel breads, oat bran muffins Semolina (regular type noodles), white flour, Barley, gluten free bread, quinoa, rice (brown or white), Spelt, semolina, sprouted wheat,	Amaranth, artichoke flour/pasta, buckwheat, CORN, couscous, cream of wheat, gluten, kasha, kamut, Popcorn, Rye (All), seven-grain, soba noodles, sorghum, shredded wheat, tapioca, teff, WHEAT, whole wheat, wild rice.
VEGETABLES	Beets, beet leaves, broccoli, Brussels Sprouts, Chinese, red, white cabbage, carrots, cauliflower, collard & mustard greens, eggplant, lima beans, parsley, parsnips, peppers (green, red, jalapeno, yellow), shitake mushrooms, sweet potatoes, yams (all)		Aloe, Domestic/Jerusalem artichokes, avocado, Juniper, olives (green, Spanish) pumpkin, radishes, rhubarb, mung, raddish sprouts, white/yellow corn, tempeh, tofu, TOMATOES

BLOOD TYPE B
Adapted from EAT RIGHT FOR YOUR TYPE
By DR. D'ADAMO

	BENEFICIAL	NEUTRAL	AVOID
FRUITS	Bananas, cranberries, grapes (black, red, green, concord), papaya, pineapple, plums (dark, red, green)	Apples, apricots, blackberries, blueberries, boysenberries, cherries (black/red), dates, elderberries, figs (dried/fresh), gooseberries, grapefruit, guava, kiwi, kumquat, lemons, limes, loganberries, mangoes, melons (cantaloupe, musk, canang, Crenshaw, honeydew, Spanish), nectarines, oranges, peaches, pears, plantains, prunes, raisins, raspberries, strawberries, tangerines	Avocado, Coconuts, persimmons, pomegranate, prickly pear, rhubarb, starfruit, bitter melon
FRUIT JUICES		ALL	
OILS	Olive	Cod liver, flax seed, walnut oil, wheat germ oil, almond oil, black, currant seed	Borage seed oil, canola, castor, coconut, corn, cottonseed, peanut, safflower, sesame, soy, sunflower
SPICES	Cayenne pepper, curry, ginger, horseradish, parsley		Acacia (Arabic gum), Allspice, almond extract, barley malt, cinnamon, corn (All), plain gelatin, black/white pepper, tapioca, Guarana
CONDIMENTS	None	Apple butter, jams & jelly from acceptable fruits, mayonnaise, mustard, sweet dill, kosher, sour pickles, relish, low fat salad dressings with acceptable ingredients	Ketchup Carrageenan, gelatin, guar gum, Miso, MSG, soy sauce, Worcestershire sauce, Almond extract, aspartame, barley malt, corn syrup, maltodextrin, stevia, sucanat
BEVERAGES	Decaf Green tea, Ginger, ginseng, licorice, parsley, peppermint, raspberry leaf, rose hips, sage	Beer, Coffee (decaf), teas (black, reg & decaf), wine (white & red), Chamomile, alfalfa, dandelion, dongquai, Echinacea, hawthorn, St Johns Wort, mint, valerian	Distilled liquor, seltzer water, soda (all types) Aloe, coltsfoot, corn silk, fenugreek, gentian, hops, linden, mullein, red clover, rhubarb, senna, shepherd's purses skullcap

Desiree Waters

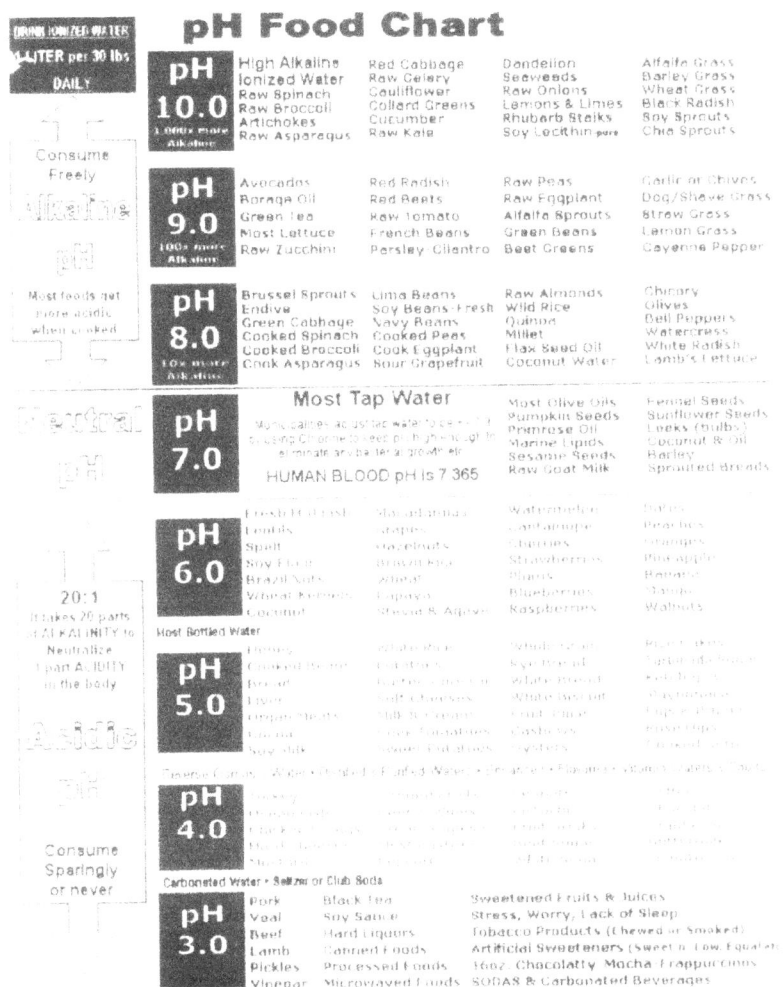

In addition to what she provided, I found other information. I needed to know where to shop, and because I am such a fussy eater that is why I had to create my own recipes.

Diet for Cancer Patients

This article was written by Paul Nison, Author/Speaker and Raw Food Gourmet Chef www.PaulNison.com – Official website of Author Paul Nison www.RawLife.com -Health E-store for all your health needs

Can diet heal cancer?

If you ask most doctors today, nothing can heal cancer. They will try to cut it out, burn it and kill it. Sometimes they have success in temporally slowing down the inevitable. The reason why they will never have a cure is because as long as the root cause is not removed, the problem will always be there.

Stress is a major root cause of cancer and must be reduced and eliminated. Removing stress from your life allows the body to do what it was designed to do; be healthy and disease free.

Where does diet come into play? Identifying stressful areas in your life is the first step toward reclaiming your health. Lack of enjoyment of life, money issues, worry, and fear build stress. But the most common stress on the body is eating and abusing harmful foods.

Abusing foods is the most common stress to the body. People consume foods that were never meant to be in our body, they eat foods in amounts that the body can't manage, and they eat at times they shouldn't be eating.

Before viewing my diet suggestions, please understand that health begins with what you eliminate from your diet, not with what you add. The first step in recovery and healing is to remove the problem foods from your diet. Then you can replace them with the healthy food you should have been eating from the beginning.

Cancer can only come alive and grow in a body that is lacking oxygen. The average person today, especially someone with cancer, is walking around with a serious case of insufficient oxygen. The following tips are musts if you are serious about overcoming cancer.

First, we will discuss what we should eliminate from our diet.

Processed foods

Eating highly processed foods prevent the body from receiving oxygen. Every bite taken from foods that come in a container, box, can, bottle or bag contributes to cancer. I tell everyone to be wary of eating these foods, especially foods without an expiration date. Healthy food is supposed to spoil after a few weeks, even a month. But if it lasts much longer, be wary. Its most likely very processed with many chemicals and other drugs to prolong the shelf life of the food while shortening the life of your body.

New Foods

If it wasn't food one hundred years ago, don't consider it food today. New foods also have new drugs and chemicals in them in amounts that are harmful to the body. Big business has created many of these foods because they care more about your wallet than your health.

Dead Foods

If you put a food in the ground and it won't grow, don't put it in your body. Foods that have their enzymes in them are known as live foods because they produce and support life. You can put the seeds of these foods into the ground and you will have a tree or plant growth. Foods that lack enzymes are known as dead foods and support death. I am a teacher at the worlds foremost health institute that specializes in healing people with cancer: Hippocrates

Health Institute (HHI) in West Palm Beach, Florida. (I highly suggest everyone with a cancer diagnosis or other health challenges go there. Mention my name for a discount). At HHI, they discovered key essentials to help the body heal itself of cancer. Two of the most common suggestions are to eat live foods with their enzymes intact and include a highly-green, chlorophyll-rich diet. Keep in mind that cooking destroys all enzymes in foods and a person trying to heal from cancer should consume a 100% raw, live-food diet.

Sugars

The directors of HHI recommend that all people healing cancer should avoid all sugars, even sugars found in fruits. Most people are aware that processed sugars are not healthful, but knowledge is lacking in regards to natural sugars, such as those found in fruits.
Regardless of the type of sugar consumed, too much sugar can cause problems. It leads to fermentation in the body that feeds and promotes yeast growth and negative bacteria. Overeating sugary foods causes constipation and gas, and this gas can back up into the bloodstream. This is where most diseases originate—from candida to cancer and everything in between. If you want to be healthy, you must learn to cut back on sugary and starchy foods.

One last tip on things to avoid: If food has to go through the car window, it definitely shouldn't be in your body.

Three things to consume if you want to overcome cancer.

1.Eating high-quality food.

If you have cancer you must treat your body the best way possible. This means only consuming food raw, ripe, fresh organic and live. Once you are healed, you can cut back to 80% of your foods meeting these criteria, but 100% is still best.

The main part of your diet should be raw vegetables and sprouts, such as leafy green vegetables, wheatgrass, algae, sea vegetables, and sunflower sprouts. The reason these green foods are so beneficial for the body is that they contain chlorophyll the blood of plants.

Chlorophyll is the pigment that gives trees, grasses, and leafy plants their characteristic, green color. More importantly, chlorophyll enables plants to convert the suns energy into nutrients that can be utilized by living organisms. Chlorophyll is similar to hemoglobin in human blood. Chlorophyll-rich, plant juices supply rich, soil-based minerals, vitamins, and chlorophyll proteins to our diet, plus it contains oxygen.

Foods high in chlorophyll include wheatgrass, which is used at health spas around the world to treat cancer and other deadly diseases, and sea algae which is available in several edible forms.

The foods you should emphasize in your diet are fresh vegetables (green vegetables are best, but others are also helpful), non-sweet fruits such as cucumbers, zucchini, bell peppers and squash. For example, cucumbers, zucchini, bell pepper, and squash are technically considered fruits because they have seeds. Because they are non-sweet fruits, they are delicious additions to the diet.

Also, in your diet should be nuts and seeds. Soaking nuts and seeds for 6 to 12 hours releases enzymes which allows for easier digestion. It's very easy to consume too many nuts, so be careful.

Whole grains and legumes can be eaten but its best to eat grains that have been sprouted first, so they are easier to digest. The least healthful grains are rye, spelt, basmati rice, white rice, wheat, barley, and corn. The most healthful grains are millet, quinoa, amaranth, tiff, buckwheat (hulled).

Of all the foods mentioned that are okay to consume, sea vegetables and sprouts are the most beneficial. These are the highest quality land and sea vegetation for our nutrients. Some popular sea vegetables are alaria, arame, dulse, hijiki, and nori.

Sprouted food is any type of seed, nut, grain, or bean that has been soaked in water, exposed to air and indirect sunlight, and if rinsed daily, has started to form a new plant, beginning with a sprout. Some examples include almond sprouts, buckwheat sprouts, sunflower sprouts and mung bean sprouts. Sprouted foods are one of the highest forms of food you can put into your body. They are very helpful for the building of new cells and provide the cells with oxygen. Green sprouts are very high in chlorophyll.

2. Eating at the right times

I just wrote a new book called The Daylight Diet (the book can be purchased at www.RawLife.com.) The point of the book is to understand that we have been designed to be on schedule if we want to be healthy!

We have all the tools we need and all the intelligence to know the best schedule for us to enjoy a healthy, long, satisfying life. Of the many ideas and concepts regarding nutrition and what foods are most nutritious for the human body, the majority of people have not taken into consideration the times of eating for best digestion.

We have been designed to eat certain foods and at certain times of the day. Just as water in your gas tank will harm the car, bad foods will harm your body. A car is made to run on certain fuel and so is our body. However, no matter what time of the day you put gas in your gas tank, it won't make a difference. The time you put fuel in your body, however, does make a big difference.

It was our Creator who first separated the salt water from the fresh, made dry land, and planted a garden. He made animals and fish before making even one human being. He provided what we needed before He even created us. If he designed our body and he knows every single hair on our heads, I'm sure he knows what we should eat and when we should eat it.

He created the heavens and the earth, including humans, food, sun, and the moon. The sun and the moon set the schedule we have been designed to follow. The information I share in this book can lead to a healthy life only if we stop watching man's calendar and clock and base our time by the sun and the moon each day.

When the sun is up, feel free to eat; when it is down, stop. I can't make this advice any simpler than that! Eat your meals as long as the sun is up, and it is light outside. But when it is dark, and the moon is rising, your meals should end for the day. This is the number one rule of the Daylight Diet. If you stick to this important principle, you will see excellent results in your health, energy, sleep your whole being because this is how we have been designed to eat. Nighttime is for resting and sleeping.

Don't eat late in the day. You will get better sleep, have better digestion, slow down the aging process, have more energy, and feel wonderful. Just stop eating late in the day especially when its dark outside and experience for yourself the great results.

Practicing temperance in eating will rejuvenate your whole body and rid you of most health problems. Your goal should be to reduce the number of meals you consume and reduce the amount of food in those meals while making sure you are consuming the highest quality food.

The real key to success is to avoid eating at night time and go to sleep on an empty stomach. Food shouldn't be a daily struggle. I can attest that it may not be easy at first, but to be truly successful, you will have to change your thinking along with your diet.

3. Eat the right way

When eating, being in a relaxed environment is very important. It is never healthy to eat when stressed no matter how good the food is. In addition, along with the amount of food, a number of meals, quality of food, and times you eat that all affect digestion, there is more that needs to be done to keep your body healthy.

After we swallow, the food we've eaten is more or less out of our control. Before that, though, we have total control:

Proper mastication and food combining can prevent many digestive problems.

Digestion begins in the mouth. Saliva contains an enzyme that helps break down the food and jumpstarts digestion. Chewing helps the body more readily extract the nutrients from the food and cuts down on the work the digestive system has to do. The less work the digestive tract has to do, the more efficiently it will do its job. When we don't chew our food well, it can ferment in our digestive system. The more food is chewed, the easier it is to digest, and the healthier it will be for the body. Even raw foods can cause problems if they're not properly chewed.

4. Food combining

The types of food we eat together, called food combining, play a big role in good digestion. Eating the wrong foods together or in the wrong order can sap our energy and cause fermenting and putrefaction in the digestive system.

Food combining allows for easier digestion and minimal digestive conflicts. It works like this: Every food takes a certain amount of time to digest. Eating similar foods with similar digestive times helps the body digest meals more easily; these foods are said to combine well. For example, watermelon takes about one hour to digest; almonds may take up to five hours. In view of this, eating watermelon and almonds at the same meal is not a good idea, so it's known as a poor combination. Eating too many meals like this may cause constipation, bloating, and gas, which may lead to more serious issues.

Final Thought

The human body is amazing when we treat it the way we're supposed to. We were designed to eat certain types of foods raw, fresh, organic fruits, vegetables, nuts, and seeds to keep our digestive systems moving and clean. Good health comes only when we have good digestion, and that good digestion only results when we eat properly and healthfully.

Stores, Foods & Recipes

Note: Read all labels because most packages, jars or containers of any product contain sugar. You will find yourself making most things from scratch, like salad dressing.

Stores:

Mom's ~ This store is organic.

Trader Joe's – Great for nuts and organic fruits (limited organic sections)

Whole Foods

Foods Options:

1 Gallon **of** water per day with ½ teaspoon lemon **or lime juice**

Matcha Green Tea

Milk: Goat's or Almond

Fresh Squeeze Juice only

Broth – Organic Vegetable or **Bone**

NO GMO FOODS ~ (Genetically Modified Organisms, which are crops developed with genetic engineering, a more precise method of plant breeding.)

Organic meats only (no pork, limited beef)

Lots of raw and oven roasted vegetables.

Homemade Soups

Cooked Greens ~ limited water and/or broth so you get total nutrients.

My Must Haves

Apple Cider Vinegar

Extra Virgin Olive Oil or Coconut Oil

Rice Crackers

Almond Butter

Himalayan Sea Salt (healthier than sea salt as it contains eighty-four minerals)

Organic seasonings

Recipes

Mayo Based Dressing

2 cups Organic Mayo

12 Tablespoons Organic Lemon Juice

12 Tablespoons White Wine Vinegar

Salt and Pepper to taste

Red Raspberry Dressing

2 small containers of Organic Fresh Raspberries

½ cup Raspberry Vinegar

1 cup Organic Olive Oil

1 squeeze Fresh Organic Lemon

Salt and Pepper to taste

Oven Roasted Veggies

Sliced Onions, Bell Peppers, Broccoli, Zucchini (Add any type of vegetables you like)

Place it in a bowl and add a light coating of Olive Oil

Add Salt, Pepper, or any other type of seasonings you like, be creative.

Place on baking sheet and cook at 350 for about 30 mins or until veggies are tender.

Three Key Health Markers and Holistic Support:

1. **pH Levels:**
   - **What it is:** pH measures the acidity or alkalinity of your body. A pH of 7 is neutral, below 7 is acidic, and above 7 is alkaline.
   - **How to test:** Use pH test strips (available at most pharmacies) to monitor your pH levels.
   - **Remember:** pH can fluctuate throughout the day, so multiple readings may be helpful.

2. **Vitamin D Levels**:
   - What it is: Vitamin D plays a crucial role in immune function, bone health, and may help protect against cancer. • Optimal levels: Aim for 30-50 ng/mL (nanograms per milliliter).
   - How to test: A simple blood test can measure your vitamin D levels.

3. **High-Sensitivity C-Reactive Protein (hs-CRP):**
   - What it is: hs-CRP is a marker of inflammation in the body, which can be linked to cardiovascular disease and other health issues.
   - How to test: Your doctor can order an hs-CRP blood test. **Holistic Supplements for Health Support:** (Always consult with your healthcare provider before starting any new supplements)
   - **Vitamin D3 (5,000 IU):** Supports immune function and may help inhibit the growth of cancer cells.

- **GTF Chromium (200 mcg):** Aids insulin function and can help manage sugar cravings.
- **Magnesium (350 mg):** Promotes muscle relaxation and stress reduction.
- **Vitamin B12 (1,000 mcg):** Essential for energy production, DNA synthesis, and red blood cell formation.
- **Vitamin C (1,000 mg):** A powerful antioxidant that may help slow cancer cell growth.
- **Vitamin K1 & K2 (550 mg):** May help protect against breast and prostate cancer.
- **Turmeric (400 mg):** A natural anti-inflammatory compound.

Important Note: This information is not intended as a substitute for professional medical advice. Always consult with your doctor, a qualified healthcare provider or an alternative doctor for personalized guidance and treatment recommendations.

Important Note for Women Considering Tamoxifen, also known as Nolvadex:

Tamoxifen is a medication used to treat certain types of breast cancer and infertility. It works by blocking estrogen receptors in the body. However, it is important to be aware that tamoxifen has potential risks and side effects.

Potential Risks and Side Effects:

- Blood clots: Tamoxifen can increase the risk of blood clots, which can lead to serious complications like stroke.
- Uterine cancer: There is a slightly increased risk of developing uterine cancer while taking tamoxifen.
- Other side effects: Hot flashes, mood changes, and vaginal dryness are also common side effects.

Alternatives to Tamoxifen:

- Estriol: Estriol is a type of estrogen that is sometimes used as an alternative to tamoxifen. However, it is important to discuss the risks and benefits of any medication with your doctor.
- Other medications: There are other medications available to treat breast cancer. Your doctor can help you determine the best option for your individual needs.

Important Considerations:

- Discuss with your doctor: Before starting any medication, it is crucial to have a thorough discussion with your doctor about the potential risks and benefits.
- Regular checkups: If you are taking tamoxifen, it is important to have regular checkups with your doctor to monitor for any potential side effects.
- Alternative therapies: Depending on your situation, alternative therapies like lifestyle changes or other medications may be appropriate.

Disclaimer: This information is not intended to be a substitute for professional medical advice. Always consult with your doctor or healthcare provider for any questions you may have about your health or treatment options. Additional Note: While tamoxifen is classified as a class 2 carcinogen by the International Agency for Research on Cancer (IARC), this classification indicates a "probable" link to cancer, not a definitive one. The decision to use tamoxifen should be made in consultation with your doctor, weighing the potential benefits against the risks.

Desiree Waters

A Special Thank You

To My Beloved Husband

To my dearest husband,

Words cannot express the depth of my gratitude for the unwavering love and support you have given me throughout my three cancer journeys. Your strength and faith have been my pillar during the most challenging times.

From the moment I received the first diagnosis, you stood by my side, holding my hand and offering me comfort. Your endless patience, your soothing words, and your gentle touch have brought me immeasurable peace. You have been my rock, my confidant, and my greatest source of strength.

During each diagnosis and treatment, you have shown remarkable resilience and an indomitable spirit. You have shouldered the burden of worry and fear with grace, allowing me to focus on healing. Your unwavering belief in my recovery gave me the courage to fight, and your love surrounded me with warmth and security.

Through the highs and lows, you have been my steadfast partner. Your ability to find joy in the small moments made me laugh when tears were close. You reminded me that the beauty of life has been a gift beyond measure. You have been my constant source of light, guiding me through the darkest days.

As we celebrate victories and reflect on the challenges, I am overwhelmed with gratitude. You have shown me the true meaning of love and partnership. Your devotion has been a beacon of hope, illuminating our path forward.

Thank you, my love, for your unwavering support, your boundless compassion, and your unshakeable faith. Together, we have faced the storm, and together, we will continue to embrace the future with faith and love.

About the Author

Desiree L. Waters

Desiree was born and raised in Baltimore, Maryland. She is a wife, mother, sister, grandmother, and great-grandmother. She graduated from Northwestern High School, attended Towson Stafford Business School and Morgan State University. She retired in November of 2023 after a wonderful, professional, and fulfilling career.

This book marks her first venture into authorship, a journey inspired by LaDonna Stanley-Thompson and the profound experiences she has. Her qualifications to write her story stem from a personal place, having been diagnosed with cancer three times. Each diagnosis brought its own set of challenges, but also profound lessons and insights.

Desiree's love for the Lord has been a pillar of strength throughout her life and significant throughout this process. It was these experiences that gave her a newfound perspective on faith and love.

Through prayer and spiritual reflection, she has discovered a deeper purpose and meaning. The collective prayers of her family, friends, and even strangers have been a beacon of hope, illuminating the dark moments and guiding her toward the light. It was through these prayers that she found the courage to face each day with renewed determination. The power of prayer has been a testament to the resilience of the human spirit and the strength that comes from being part of a loving and supportive community.

As she reflects on her journey, she is grateful for the outpouring of prayers and the impact they had on her life. It is through the kindness and compassion of others that she has been able to navigate the challenges faced while battling cancer.

Contact: DWCancerJourney@gmail.com

Part 3:

When the Highway of Happiness Forces You to Take an Unexpected Detour

by Karen Hargrove

When the Highway of Happiness Forces You to Take an Unexpected Detour

Karen Hargrove

I was on the highway of happiness. I had graduated from college, married my college sweetheart, we both were employed, and we had our apartment. Two years in and my husband and I decided we were ready to become parents. I remember telling my family physician, my husband and I are ready to start our family. His response was, "great." He indicated that it will probably take a year to conceive given the time frame I had been using contraceptives. I should have placed a wager because within a few months I was pregnant. Yes, the happy couple was enjoying total happiness. I was so loving this highway. Nine months later my husband and I were blessed with a beautiful baby girl. Our life as a family was just beginning. Life couldn't have been any better as we navigated this highway of life full of joy. Now I am not I to believe there will not be trouble along the way. You know a little sickness here and there, financial setbacks due to an unexpected expense, the death of a loved one, you know the "normal" stuff. Well, 18 months after our daughter Jamiece was born there was a caution sign up ahead, directing us to detour. Normally, when one sees a detour sign it's usually due to construction of some sort and all vehicles must exit. This was a strange detour because my family was the only vehicle exiting from the highway of happiness. All the other vehicles kept going.

One day, I am in the shower, and I feel this lump, or rather, see this lump on my breast. I had just had my annual physical and received a clean bill of health just probably two months prior. Now I am not one to wait around when it comes to my health or my family's health, so, we went to the doctor immediately and he examined my breast and recommended I see a specialist. Initially, it didn't click the doctor he had recommended was a breast cancer specialist. Before my appointment with the specialist the lump had grown. Fortunately, my doctor is not only a breast cancer specialist who has done extensive breast cancer studies outside the country; including Asia; but he is also grounded in the same faith and religion as me. The specialist took some measurements and proceeded to ask me some questions. He also scheduled a biopsy, and afterwards, I began the week-long wait for the results.

I went to the doctor alone to find out my results from the biopsy. The nurse came in and asked if I had come alone. I said yes because I was planning to go back to work, and she went back out. I remember feeling like I sat in that examination room on that table for at least 30 minutes before the nurse returned with the doctor. You see, not only was I anxious to get my result but so was my mother. She and my father were aware of my appointment and were expecting my call telling them everything was good. The doctor said, "Karen we have your results back and it's malignant." I look at him and said, "OK, what does that mean?" He says, "You have Stage 1 Breast Cancer." The unexpected, dreaded detour from the highway of happiness was CANCER!

After the shock I could no longer hear anything, the doctor was saying because I was crying and had pretty much checked out mentally. I was thinking of death, who's going to take care of my baby? What will my husband do, how will he cope? The doctor leaves but the nurse stays with me. She was so kind; her name was Rachel. I will never forget her name. Rachel asked who I wanted her to call. I asked her to call my husband. At this point I feel as if I am alone on this detour. I remember Rachel calling my husband's school and telling him it was an emergency, and he needed to get here Immediately.

It took my husband at least 45 minutes to an hour to get to me. He did not work in the county we resided in at the time. I also told Rachel (the nurse) to call my parents, they also were an hour and a half away. After waiting for what seemed like an eternity my husband arrives, and I am still sobbing, but I no longer feel alone. My rock, my better half and protector had arrived. James (my husband) was hugging me asking what was wrong. In between my sobs I managed to say it was cancer. I will never forget this moment as long as I live; one tear from James' eye fell and landed on my wrist directly on my pulse point where it was absorbed into my skin. Nothing is more heart wrenching than seeing your man cry. I felt comforted and at peace at that moment because I knew (which I never doubted) he was with me 100% on this awful detour. I also knew we would pick up supporting passengers along the way. We left the doctor's office and went home, and my parents arrived shortly after. My supervisor called because I told her I would be returning to work. While on the phone, I started crying again and my

Supervisor, Sharon said, "It's ok Karen call me when you can," and she gave me her personal number. I remember my mom hugging me so tight I could not breathe. I laughed while she was hugging me. Leave it to me to always find laughter somewhere. Remember I said I would pick up passengers as I journeyed on this detour, well I picked up my two sisters Cassie and Pam, my aunts, other family members, in-laws, and friends. I received so many encouraging words, scriptures, and prayers along the way.

It Is important for me to mention that breast cancer did not run in my family, and I went through a bout of being angry. Someone obviously had cancer and did not share it with the family. I began questioning my mother because she was adopted by family members and knew her biological family. Afterall it would have had to come from my mom's side of the family. Why I thought that I had no idea. Probably because I did not know of anyone having breast cancer on my father's side and the only unknown was my mother's biological immediate family. I guess I was looking for the why behind it; you know, in my genetic background. We could not pinpoint genetically how I was the chosen one to be diagnosed with cancer. I had single-handedly changed our family's medical history. When visiting a doctor and they ask about medical history, my family now must check the box on cancer. I was the one chosen to alter our family medical history. Way to go, Karen! I will later reveal why I believe I was the chosen one.

It was now time for action. Another moment I will never forget; my older sister, Cassie, came down from Maryland to accompany me, my husband, and my parents to my doctor's appointment. The appointment turned into a full-blown round robin discussion with my sister taking charge. She pulled out this planner with questions, statistics, notes, and probably some handouts too. By the time the appointment was ending the doctor asked If I had any additional questions. He also said I had a great support system in place. When we left the appointment, I knew the procedure I would undergo, date, time, location, as well as the treatment that would follow surgery, which would be chemotherapy. My sister was on point that day.

Yes, I had a great support system on this detour but at the end of the day it is me getting my body altered. The part of my body society says makes you sexy. (Thank God my husband is not a breast man); you know the hourglass figure every woman initially desires to have. Then there is the high possibility you will lose your hair. OK ladies, how do we feel about our hair? We spend hours in hair salons, tons of money on clothes and makeup to enhance our beauty. Who doesn't want to look beautiful? We all do. Well ladies and gentlemen, cancer will change your whole perspective on "stuff" you believe makes you who you are. Cancer will humble you and force you to get in tune with your inner being. Trust me, you no longer sweat the small stuff. Cancer and the treatment will temporarily change your appearance, and it will disrupt your mind-set. This is the detour "you" must tarry through. Does it affect family? Yes, it does! Remember I was a new mommy. I cannot imagine what my husband, parents, siblings, and close friends were experiencing and how they were coping. Who did they talk to about their fears of losing me? I had the fear of dying because of what I was leaving behind...loved ones. I called my best friend from college to inform her, and she started crying. She had an aunt diagnosed with breast cancer. I am sure my news rekindled the distress her family experienced. Cancer impacts everyone in your circle.

Let's talk about the good, the bad, and the ugly of my chemotherapy treatment. After my surgery altered my body, the next step was the treatment. My treatment was to be for six months biweekly. My routine included leaving work early on Fridays to arrive at the oncologist's office, sitting in a comfortable recliner to get hooked up to an IV to receive my chemotherapy. The process would take about an hour and a half. I would be given lemon-lime soda and lemon or cinnamon candy to offset the nausea and awful taste in my mouth. To this day, I cannot and will not drink any lemon lime-flavored soda. After my treatment, my husband would pick me up and we would return Saturday morning to pick up my car. It did not take long to experience the effects of this medicine/cocktail better known as chemo. My skin became dull, my fingernails and toenails darkened, my arms had track marks from the needles, my appetite went out the window, and short-term memory was not as sharp. Despite it all, I did not lose my hair. Can you tell I love my hair? Yes, I love my hair!

There is a new sign ahead and it says, Detour Ending. I, along with my family and other supporting riders are now exiting back onto the highway of happiness. I have a new attitude and a new outlook on life, and nothing will stress me out. I have never had self-esteem issues; in fact, my self-esteem has always been off the charts thanks to my mom Instilling morals and values in her children. My new mantra was: "Don't nobody bring me no bad news." Followed by the question, Is it that serious? My new attitude got on my mom's nerves because I had a positive outlook on everything and I understand sometimes people want to have their moment of feeling down or blue, well honey I was not the one to come to if you were trying to stay in that space. Life is too short, and I was given another opportunity at life to do something differently and I was going to do just that. Did I still have my moments of not so good days, of course I did. Here's one for you, I recall my oncologist wanted us to wait at least five years before conceiving again due to the after-effects of chemo. I am the co-captain of my life. The captain is far from what the eye can see; a higher being, and He said no. Along comes my son Xavian, and he is healthy at 8 lbs. Born a year before my anniversary of being cancer free. Yes, I had my moment of fear. I did not know if my unborn baby would suffer from the after-effects of chemo or if the cancer would return. Let's just say this, I am fully grounded in my faith-based belief, but when you are hit with cancer all your religion, faith, and spirituality go right out the window. If anyone says something different then they are not being truthful with you. I will tell you this, it all comes back quickly. My favorite scripture is Isaiah 54:17, which says, "No weapon that is formed against me shall prosper." Whenever I am faced with adversaries, sadness, stress, anxiety, or anything detrimental to my physical health or mental health, I repeat this verse out loud. Remember, I said breast cancer did not run in my family, and I wanted to know why I was the chosen one. Three years after I was diagnosed, my mom was diagnosed with breast cancer but guess what; we were ready this time around. We knew what to expect. I was my mom's anchor providing the strength she needed to get through her journey on her unexpected detour. I believe that was my purpose for going through this. Honestly speaking, if it was up to me, I would have chosen another way to be a beacon of hope to my mom. My unexpected detour had ended; myself and all my passengers accompanying me are now merging back onto the highway of happiness.

The highway of happiness is a beautiful highway. Yes, there will be potholes, construction, and road closures along the way, but we keep it moving. Life continues. The expected things you encounter in life will show up, i.e., marriage, birth of a baby, death of a loved one, financial hardship, loss of a job, or even general sicknesses such cold and flu. But is anyone ever ready for the unexpected detour of cancer…AGAIN!?

Over twenty years later, I went for an annual mammogram. I've done these procedures several times, so going alone has never been an issue for me. The results were always the same…good. The month was December. It's the holiday season so, tis the season to be jolly, spread good cheer and give. After the mammogram, the technician has my image and shares it with the doctor. The technician comes back in and says the doctor wants me to take another image. No worries, I have dense tissues and sometimes my images aren't clear. After, the technician takes that second image, they come again and says the doctor wants to see you. Now I am having a conversation with myself. Are you kidding and here I am again…alone. That's the clean version of my dialogue with myself. Ok, back to the doctor. She says, "Karen I am concerned about this spot and given your history, (which I am beginning to hate at this point) I want to do a biopsy." Thank goodness I took the day off. See what I learned from the last episode? Well obviously, not quite because I came by myself...again. I have the biopsy and this time the results come back within an hour or two. It's malignment! I have been diagnosed with cancer again and this time in my right breast. Had I known this was going to happen I would have had a double mastectomy and reconstruction 20 years ago! This time I can hear everything the doctor is saying. I do not check out, not fully anyway, but I am thinking of the holidays. To give you some perspective on why I am thinking of the holidays and how bad the timing was; as if there is good timing for a cancer diagnosis; for the past few Christmas holidays, I would host Christmas dinner and post-Christmas brunch and this Christmas I was hosting again. It is what I do. Believe it or not, by this time I am not paying attention to what the doctor is saying, I just have hosting dinner on the brain. Then it hits me, "Oh no chemo again and my hair. Will I lose my hair?"

After leaving the office I am standing on the corner trying to compose self as I call my sister Cassie first. I knew she was off from work every other Friday, but I got her voicemail. I did not call my husband James at first because he was at work, and I did not want to give him this news while he was at work like I had to do the last time. I think it's awful to receive bad news at work. Unless someone is transitioning hold the news. Next, I called my neighbor Althea, and of course I am crying as I tell her because I must go through this again. My sister called me back and I asked her where she was because I really wanted her to come to my doctor's office, but she was at the hair salon. I proceeded to tell her my news. Then it hit me again, "Oh no my HAIR. Will I lose my hair? Why couldn't my sister be at the nail salon instead?"

I am still crying and trying to compose myself because I am on M street just outside of the doctor's office. Yes, I am in DC. I do remember telling my sister I am not afraid of cancer, I am dreading going through chemo again, it's an experience you hope never to have to repeat. After sharing with my sister, I drove home wondering what lesson I had not learned, that I must go through this ordeal again and how or when do I break the news to hubby and our two grown kids both of which are away in college. My daughter was a senior, (graduating in May) and our son was a freshman. My husband comes home, and I break the news to him. He hugs me and tells me we will get through it together.

Welcome to my second unexpected detour (cancer), it is not a detour I would wish on anyone. We decided to tell our kids when they came for winter break. I begin with, "I have some bad news, I have been diagnosed with breast cancer again." My daughter cries and responded, "This is supposed to be happy times." Remember, it is December, and I host Christmas dinner and brunch, and we always have a blast. We cook, eat, share memories, take selfies, take pictures, laugh together and exchange gifts. I totally understood my daughter's response because I was having the same thoughts. I reassured her this will be a joyous occasion. My son, Mr. Cool and Calm reiterated what my husband said we will get through it together, and everything will be fine. The holidays came and went, and we then shared the news with extended family members. It was time to start another mile or two on this second unexpected detour through surgery and chemotherapy treatment.

This time around I have a new team of doctors and new friends sharing this journey with me. My medical care would take place at George Washington Hospital in Washington, DC. My team of doctors consisted of a breast care doctor, oncologist, and reconstruction specialist. My team of doctors and I decided the best course of action would be to have my treatment first then follow with the reconstruction surgery. Can you guess the first question I asked the oncologist? Come on, say it with me; "Will I lose my hair?" The second question I asked was "Will I receive the chemo known as the red devil?" The answer to both questions was yes. In fact, she said I would lose my hair within 10 days (about 1 and a half weeks) of starting chemo.

Back to my new passengers that accompanied me on the second journey. I was a part of a group that originally consisted of 10 ladies. This group worked out together, took trips to New York to see plays on Broadway, traveled to Mexico, celebrated our children's graduations, and started a book club. The book club was my idea, (ok, that was my pat on the back.) But I must give credit to our girl Antoinette. She came up with the name of our book club (Books with Friends). May she rest in peace. It was at our book club that I shared that I was diagnosed with breast cancer. These ladies gathered in a circle and prayed. It is a moment I will never forget. At that moment I knew these sister/friends were with me on the detour. The book club now consists of seven ladies: Karen (KB), Althea, Val, Paulette, Pauline, Stacey, and I would make the seventh. This group is special and unique. Trust me, with seven different personalities that can and do get on each other's nerves but will come together when needed, yes, we are unique and special. It's the personalities that make us so unique and fit together. I have given these ladies nick names. Karen (KB) could be called the mother of the group because she has this mother look she gives us when we misbehave, and we misbehave a lot. KB is also the baker in the group. We love her poundcake. I also love her homemade cinnamon rolls. Next there's Althea (The Motivator) because she will have you doing things you do not want to do and will not let up until you do it. We also have Val (The Quiet Storm). She only speaks when required and what she says is always on point. Paulette and Pauline (The Twins). I do not know them apart and it's been more than 15 years. They are always correcting each other, and one is supposedly nicer than the other, but I don't know which one. Then there is Stacey (The Wine Connoisseur). She is the youngest in the group and is always getting into trouble so we will leave it there. Put us all together and you have a unique and special group of ladies.

Ok back to the chemotherapy treatment, while I was getting my first round of chemo, Stacey and Antoinette were with me. The IV was put into my arm and the red devil was administered. Apparently, my body did not like the red devil cocktail because I had a reaction the minute it hit my bloodstream. I broke out in hives and was given a strong dose of antihistamine and sent home. Stacey took me to a few more treatments and took me to pick up stuff I would need from CVS. I am forever grateful. My oldest sister Cassie would round out the last couple treatments with me. Cassie was with me when I rang the bell signaling the last round of my chemo.

This treatment of Chemo was totally different from my last treatment. I had a chemo port put in to allow the chemo to be delivered directly into the vein without the need for needles. I experienced neuropathy in my toes and fingers. I was tired and my stamina had diminished. Walking up steps was a chore, and I had this awful pain in my back. I had a device on my arm which would administer medication preventing me from feeling nauseated. The nurse advised me to take Claritin before my treatment. Who knew an allergy pill would alleviate my back pain.

Now please allow me to share the mental and physical anguish I experienced during my treatment on this unexpected detour. I lost my hair. My skin completion darkened as well as my nails and the palms of my hand. I lost my appetite. I received a list of things I could not do from a session I attended. The list indicated no pedicures or manicures, when having intercourse use a condom (I was thinking, "Are you kidding me? I'm freaking married.") You are probably asking why. When you receive chemo, your immune system is compromised therefore you must be careful at all costs, even to avoid excessive time in the sun. I even received a coupon for a free wig. For the first time as an adult, I felt unattractive. I remember leaving the session and having a good cry.

Yes, I had a moment, but I quickly bounced back. After the 10 days of chemo, my hair came out, I went to my stylist, and she shaved my head. I came home, put on my makeup and earrings and I was rocking my bald head. Unfortunately, I suffer from porosis and seborrheic dermatitis which is pretty much a buildup of dry skin. So, I could not rock the baldness, but I was rocking the headwraps. I had one in every color. I really did not care for wigs. I only had two and I seldom wore them.

My last treatment was the week of my daughter's college graduation. The graduation would take place outside in a stadium and that day in May was hot. Remember I stated the oncologist said to avoid excessive time in the sun, well I was not going to miss my baby's graduation. I felt horrible. I had an umbrella to use but the use of it was prohibited. My sister Cassie loaned me her hat. My sister-in-law was fanning me, and my cousin Crystal bought a frozen drink. Now I knew why my doctor said avoid the sun. It will shut your body down, but I got through it, and it was a beautiful celebration.

We are now at the last leg of this unexpected detour, yes, surgery. I elected to have a mastectomy and reconstruction at the same time. The doctors provided me with the date, and I politely told them the July date would not work because my cousin was getting married, and I wanted to go to the wedding. I am saddened to say I missed the wedding. The procedure was 14 hours. The best sleep of my life. Now I do not have any issues with the procedures, but I loathe the recovery/healing process; the pain, the medication, being immobile, waking up in the middle of the night and needing assistance, yes, all that stuff.

Karen Hargrove

Fortunately, my husband James and my mommy (yes, we call our mother mommy) were there to assist with recovery as well as other family members and friends. My sister/friend KB came over with a pan of homemade chicken potpie (without peas because she knows I hate peas), homemade cinnamon rolls and a pan of homemade rolls. I had my phone group set up by a church member (Rita) consisting of other ladies battling cancer. As you can see, I was never alone on this detour. I picked up a bunch of new passengers.

The cancer club Is something no one signs up for but when you are selected, by no choice of your own, you are forced to alter your life on the unexpected detour. I was selected when my daughter was 18 months, and I guess my membership expired because it was renewed during my daughter's last year in college. It impacts not only you, but your circle of family friends and you find yourself digging deep for that inner strength. My strength was my family and my faith. I had to raise my daughter and be there for her college graduation. We all have it. Because I am a breast cancer survivor, I have duties and responsibilities. I must remind ladies to get mammograms (don't go alone) make it date with your spouse, partner, friend or whomever and do those monthly self-breast checks (yes touch your breast). It is my duty to share my story because one never knows who needs to hear it. It is my responsibility to stand in for those whose body just could not fight any longer and continue the fight for resources and research to find a cure for this awful disease. Cancer humbles you. I no longer sweat the small stuff (not much) because I will check you if I feel the need. I listen more

Karen Hargrove

(still working on talking less) I put myself first (most of the time). It's ok to say no. I tell my immediate family I love them every day. My faith has been renewed, and I am mentally stronger. Life is too short so you had better live your life to the fullest because you do not know when that detour sign will pop up ahead. If or when it pops up on your highway of happiness, look me up, I will travel it with you, after all it is my duty and responsibility.

Acknowledgments

First and foremost, I must give thanks to my Heavenly Father for being with me and preparing me even before this journey began. To the love of my life, my husband James Hargrove, my daughter Jamiece and son Xavian, for supporting me in more ways than you will ever know.

To my mother (RIP), who was with me through both detours and as well as my two sisters Cassie and Pam. Special shout out to my big sister for accompanying me to my treatments.

To my Books with Friends book club – Karen, Althea, Pauline, Paulette, Val and Stacey. Thanks for the food (KB), taking me to my treatments Antoinette (RIP) and Stacey, and for the cleaning service, thank you Paulette.

To my church members at Fort Washington Baptist Church, especially my choir members, go Altos. A special shout out to Deacon Wallace, from day one, you told me I had a story to tell.

To my bestie, Phoebe, thanks for listening when I had my moments.

To all my extended family, in-laws and friends, thanks for walking with me on this detour. Last but certainly not least, thank you LaDonna for the ask. We are forever connected.

About the Author

Karen Hargrove

Karen Hargrove resides in Upper Marlboro Maryland, and she is a two-time breast cancer survivor. She has compassion for those going through the battle of cancer and passionately shares her story with the hope of uplifting their spirits. She is a consultant for a private company. Karen is a proud alumna of Winston-Salem State University and holds a Bachelor of Science degree in political science. She holds a Master of

Science degree in public administration from North Carolina Central University. She is a member of Fort Washington Baptist Church in Fort Washington Maryland. Karen is married to her college sweetheart, James who is an awesome father and husband. From their union of over 30 years, they have a beautiful daughter, Jamiece, and a handsome son, Xavian. Karen enjoys reading, singing, traveling, and hanging out with her sister/friends.

Part 4:

Cancer!?

Never Crossed My Mind

by DeWayne Perry

Cancer!?
Never Crossed My Mind

DeWayne Perry

August 2017, I was routinely busy as usual maintaining a full-time job doing Facility Management work for the Federal Government and owning and operating a part time heating and air conditioning business. August, being one of the hottest months, brings a demanding schedule. While managing both careers, running from sunup to sundown, I noticed I was having issues with my stomach and more specifically, my digestive system. I had a normal appetite for food, but it seemed that after I ate, my food just kind of "sat in my chest" and would not process as normal. Then, I would get a feeling that I could only describe as contractions, as if I could feel the food moving through my digestive system very slowly. For me, this was highly unusual as I never have stomach discomfort unless I'm about to be sick.

Well of course, when I first noticed it, I "blew it off" and thought it would pass, but over the following weeks it only got worse. Then, the day before we were to take my youngest daughter to college, which happened to be a very big deal because she's somewhat introverted and a "homebody" and she was going to school two and a half hours away from home in Frostburg, MD. I decided to invite some family and friends over for her last night home. I ordered pizza and chicken wings as a light meal with refreshments. While working earlier that day I ate very little, but

I was drinking ginger ale and water trying to relieve what felt like gas discomfort in my chest. At the end of the busy day, I picked up the pizza and wings shortly before our guest arrived, placed them in the kitchen and went off to shower and get cleaned up. After using the restroom, I happened to look back into the toilet which I rarely do, and I noticed there were some blood droplets in the water. This caused me to somewhat panic as I had never experienced that before. I immediately showered with my mind racing about what I would do next. By the time I was done getting showered and dressed I had determined that I needed to excuse myself from our guest and go to the emergency room or urgent care facility to get checked.

I pulled my wife to the side, told her what happened and then discretely exited alone to seek treatment and or a diagnosis. When I saw the doctor at the local urgent care facility, he ran all the routine tests and blood work which came back normal. During this process, he asked me if I had had a colonoscopy. I told him no, but I was planning to do so since I had turned fifty that year. This was the age that I had always heard that men needed to have this procedure done. I vividly remember his disappointment and response like, "Come on bro, really? You should have had than done by now." I was a bit puzzled because I was always under the impression that 50 was the age for your first colonoscopy. I also saw my primary care doctor annually and he never mentioned getting it done earlier. At any rate, after his examination he recommended that I see a gastroenterologist and get the procedure done as soon as possible. This was a Friday evening, so I couldn't contact my primary care physician until the next Monday. My biggest concern at this point was whether I could load all my daughters' belongings up, travel, get all her belongings unloaded and into her dormitory the following day. As a father, I certainly did not want this to be led and or done by anyone other than me.

After returning home from the urgent care facility, I exchanged pleasantries with my mother, sister and in-laws, but made light of my medical condition to keep them from being alarmed. You see, I am surrounded by women, my wife, two daughters, mother, sister, mother in-law, sister in-law, and two nieces. This is a good thing, but I knew it would emotionally upset them and I didn't want to ruin the moment in any type of way, especially since I had no real answers. My dad was alive then, but he wasn't at my house that night. Of course, I ate very little, if at all that night to minimize my discomfort. I had started this practice weeks prior when I was trying to figure things out and "self-medicate." I went to bed and prayed asking God to give me the strength to be able to get my daughter moved the next morning and just like I asked, He did so. They were all aware that I was not feeling well but not alarmed that it was anything major.

After getting her settled into her new home, we returned home and resumed our daily life activities. On that Monday, I contacted my primary care doctor to arrange a colonoscopy. He made the referral for me, but it was going to be about two weeks before the gastroenterologist could see me for the initial consultation. I made that appointment and anxiously waited for its arrival. During this period, I continued to eat less, and I would have less discomfort or pain by doing so. Well of course that came with its own consequences such as less energy and rapid weight loss. This appointment could not come fast enough. The following weekend was Labor Day weekend, and I was dragging. I was functioning but feeling generally horrible and weak. On Labor Day morning, I decided to get dressed and go to the Emergency Room to see if I could see a gastroenterologist at the hospital. I did exactly that but after several hours in what I remember as a freezing cold emergency room, the doctor said there was nothing they could do because my situation was not an emergency. I returned home disappointed and dejected.

My appointment with the gastroenterologist was a few days after my visit to the "ER." When I finally got there, he confirmed that I needed the colonoscopy and set it up for the following week. He was able to prescribe me a medication that helped with the stomach discomfort and allowed me to eat a bit more and gain some strength back. After having the colonoscopy procedure done the following week, I recall waking up groggy in the recovery area where my wife helped me to get dressed. The doctor came in shortly after with digital photos of my colon and said that he removed a couple of small polyps but there was a tumor in my colon near my appendix that was causing the problems that I was having and that from the "looks of it" (darkly colored) it could very well be cancerous. Me, still being buzzed from the anesthesia was stunned but grateful that there was at least a diagnosis. I was like okay, what's next and when? He told us that he would have to get me scheduled for surgery as soon as possible and that the tumor would be removed and then tested to see if it was cancerous. I was referred to a surgical oncologist at the Washington Hospital Center in Washington, DC and in early October, I had surgery which removed the tumor and thirteen inches of my colon and my appendix. This procedure is known as a colectomy.

This was all quite an experience for me since I had never spent one night in a hospital before. Two days after the surgery, I was released from the hospital and went home to recover. The recovery went relatively well. I didn't do much but sit in my recliner and heal as I was advised. I had some pain from where the incision was made for about a week and then that subsided. I began to eat regularly and started to take walks to build up my stamina and strength. About a week later, I got the call from Dr. Fitzgerald, my surgeon oncologist. It was at this time he confirmed that the tumor was cancerous and that I had a condition called Large B Cell Lymphoma which is rare for a 50-year-old black man, but rather most found in 80-year-old white men. It's a blood cancer that just so happened to reveal itself in the soft tissue of my colon. It was not what is commonly known as colon cancer. I recall being disappointed, but the fact that the gastroenterologist thought that the tumor might have been cancerous may have softened this blow.

Once again, my attitude was, what do we have to do next? Having to share this news with loved ones was uncomfortable, especially my youngest daughter who was watching her best friend's father go through tremendous adversity while being treated for cancer. We decided to keep it from her for several weeks but, on her first trip home from school she came into my bedroom and saw me resting in bed, which is unusual, and she came right out and asked, "What's wrong with you?" I told her as gently as I could that I had a form of cancer that I was going to need to be treated for. She immediately burst into tears, and we consoled each other as we embraced. I let her know that everything was going to be okay. My oldest daughter was living at home and aware of the process step by step. She also had medical background and was vigorously growing in her relationship with God at the time, so she was rock solid and bossing me around like a nurse! However, a few years later she revealed that she wasn't as stable as she projected at the time and that she had thoughts about the possibility of losing her father to cancer.

Because it was blood cancer, I needed to be referred to a hematologist next. Dr. Fitzgerald referred me to one of his colleagues, but he was not available, so I was then referred to Dr. Vera Malkovska. A tough, European straight-shooting physician with a no-nonsense attitude but a good disposition and bedside manner. A few weeks later my wife and I met with Dr. Malkovska, and she arranged for me to take a battery of tests to include a CAT Scan, PET Scan, and a spinal tap. Well, I was most worried about the discomfort associated with the spinal tap, but I prayed earnestly and by God's grace, it ended up being relatively painless. Hallelujah!

After I had completed all the tests, we met again and she stated that the cancer had not spread anywhere else but, because this form of cancer can be aggressive, she did recommend that I undergo six treatments of strong chemotherapy as a precaution. These treatments would take place once every twenty-one days. She thoroughly explained the process to my wife and I and explained the effects or impacts that would take place because of the treatment. Things such as fatigue, hair loss, lack of energy, loss of libido, weight loss, loss of taste, etc. I was then also connected with all the programming that the Washington Hospital Cancer Treatment Center had to offer. They have several support groups and resources available to patients in treatment for cancer. I was very fortunate to have supportive immediate family and close friends, as well as a loving Pastor and church family. While I did not take advantage of the additional resources the hospital offered, they were certainly available to me.

The Cancer Center even has a program where volunteers knit blankets to give to patients to keep warm during chemo and at home. This was a very nice and thoughtful gesture. I think it brought more comfort to my wife than to me. Additionally, I learned that these programs are especially beneficial for people who don't have family and support systems. When going through this process you realize that cancer does not discriminate. You see all ages, races, and genders in treatment.

I was given a choice regarding the chemo treatment. Since the cancer was not found anywhere else, I could have done nothing, but since it was recommended that I complete the treatment due to the nature of Large B-Cell Lymphoma, I chose to proceed. After doing so, I was referred to the Hospital Center's chemotherapy class. Here you learn about chemo and the process for the treatment. Given that my treatment would be intravenous it was recommended that I get a device called a port placed in my chest that would serve as the connecting point for the needle needed to give me the treatments. This would require another surgical procedure that placed the small pouch in my upper left chest. This device has a tube that runs from it to the jugular vein in your neck. Using this device helps the medication to get into your bloodstream properly. Installing the port was an in and out surgical procedure that was painless, however, the chest area directly over the port was very sore for a week or two.

Within two weeks of getting the port, my treatment began. This required that I go to the cancer center infusion lab where I sat in a reclining chair watching TV for several hours while I received five different IV medications, one bag at a time. The first of these treatments caused me the most discomfort. Immediately following it, I got chills on the way home and shortly after getting home, I became quite nauseous and uncomfortable with vomiting. After consulting with the on-call doctor that night, I almost went back to the hospital but instead, I prayed and went to bed for the night. I felt better the following morning, however, nowhere near normal.

When I shared this experience with my doctor, she stated that I should not have gotten sick as this is a rare occurrence with modern treatments. She had me change the order of taking my oral medication and eating before I received my treatments, and I experienced no sickness issues following those treatments. After my second or third treatment, I noticed that I was losing my hair. I would begin to see loose hairs on my shirt and clothing. This continued to progress, and I lost all my body hair.

I was already a bald man so there was no issue there but soon after, there was no mustache, beard or eyebrows which was weird. I had been told to expect it and that it would return after the treatments stopped. Outside of an occasional bad taste in my mouth, the only other noticeable effect was feeling tired or worn down. I would describe it as me feeling like I just wanted a hug.

I was fortunate to have an employer that understood the situation and they allowed me to telework throughout the treatment process. This was a tremendous blessing because while in treatment, your immune system gets heavily weakened, and it's not recommended that you be around people unnecessarily. As a result, I had to surrender my HVAC service work to my business partner. I could not attend family functions or social gatherings or church. My duties as church musician had to be shared by the other musicians. For the first time in my life, I had to just sit still and focus on resting and heeling.

I completed my 6th and final treatment on March 1, 2018, my wife's birthday. When I returned home that day, my oldest daughter Alex surprised me with flowers, a card, and a 6-foot banner hanging up that read "I beat Cancer." I still have that banner hanging in my closet however, I take no credit for the victory. It was the work of the Lord! A few weeks later my wife and I took a celebratory trip to Florida where she got to attend the Miami Open Tennis Tournament, and I got to go fishing. It was a great trip that allowed us to treat ourselves after going through this eight-month ordeal.

Never did I expect this to be a part of my life story, especially at the age of 50. I was quite athletic up until my late twenties and have always been relatively active and healthy. Even when I first started to feel bad, I was certain it was something minor. Cancer never crossed my mind. Certainly, this was another life lesson for me. I thank God that I already had a close relationship with Him and that this was an opportunity to exercise the faith that I had been professing to have. He provided me with peace throughout the entire process. I can honestly say that I was more concerned about the discomfort that I would feel from the treatments and testing than I was anything else. Within my spirit, I was content and trusting in Him knowing everything was going to be okay either way.

Now that I have had this experience, I share my story with others who are going through similar circumstances. I take the time to check on them and encourage them and let them know that a cancer diagnosis is not a death sentence. I'm constantly encouraging my male counterparts to go to the doctor regularly and get the colonoscopy and prostate checkups when recommended or even sooner if possible. I find that people are extremely grateful for this.

You never know what you will have to go through in life but through it all we must persevere. I am so grateful to have a loving and caring wife by my side who was relentless with attending appointments with me and even sleeping at the hospital, even when I told her I didn't need her to. She and my daughters catered to my every need through the process which is not surprising because they generally do so. I appreciate this even more when I think about so many people who don't have anyone to be there for them during difficult and challenging times such as this. I can't imagine being one of those people.

After treatment completion, I had to see my doctor on sixty, ninety, and one hundred twenty-day intervals for a while until it became an annual visit. When doing so, I go to the Washington Hospital Cancer Center and sit in the waiting room with patients that are actively getting treatment. It's a humbling experience every time I walk up to that building. It reminds me to take nothing for granted. Tomorrow is not promised! But it also reminds me to give thanks to an almighty God for His grace and mercy each and every day!

About the Author

DeWayne Perry

DeWayne Perry is a native Washingtonian who grew up in the far southwest area of the city. Born to James and Donna Perry in 1967, he was educated in the District of Columbia School System. Following graduation from FW Ballou high School in 1984 he attended the Lincoln Technical Institute studying Heating, Ventilation and Air Conditioning (HVAC). After successfully completing this training, he became employed by the Federal Government where he served for 38 years with the General Services Administration, The Smithsonian, The National Park Service and The Federal Housing Finance Agency. DeWayne retired from federal service in December of 2023, but he continues to operate a small HVAC business which he has owned and operated for over 30 years.

DeWayne has been married for 35 years to his wife Shelia, and they have two beautiful daughters, Alexandra (30) and Drew (25). He also serves faithfully at the Ft Washington Baptist Church in Ft Washington Maryland where he serves as an ordained deacon, musician, choir member and Sunday School teacher. When not working or serving in church, he enjoys the outdoors, music, sports, fishing, hunting, boating and riding his motorcycle.

Part 5:

Atomic Prayer

Combating Cancer Through Prayer

by Kenyette Spencer

Atomic Prayer
Combating Cancer Through Prayer

Kenyette Spencer

If you are reading this book, perhaps you or someone that you love has been diagnosed with cancer. Be encouraged! There is hope beyond what you see. There is hope beyond the diagnoses! Through faith, healthy living, and proper medical attention, it is possible not just to survive a cancer diagnosis, but to thrive and to live a healthy and bountiful life!

I can tell from experience that the most important thing you can do is to remain positive. Let the joy of the Lord be your strength!

If we were gathered around a table, I would listen as you shared your story. I would applaud you for your courage, faith, and strength in God. I'd tell you my testimony about how God guarded my steps and rebuked the hand of the enemy who tried to overwhelm me with sorrow, defeat, and depression.

I'd tell you that not every season lasts forever, but every season does produce something precious, even if it's just a fresh perspective.

I'd tell you that sometimes God gives us just enough light for the step we are on. Just keep walking in faith the dust will eventually settle, and the storm will soon pass.

I'd tell you that I learned to stay humble, forgive quickly, and show others a lot of grace and love along the way.

I'd tell you that I've learned to apologize often and to take the wisdom I've learned to do better next time. I'd tell you that I've learned to guard my heart and my tongue and keep them pure.

I'd tell you that God is truly all we will ever need. He is our SUSTAINER, PROVIDER, HEALER, and FRIEND. He will send others that will be the very expression of His heart towards you.

I'd tell you that I learned the importance of appreciating all the beauty around me. People heal when they are loved well. I'd tell you that YOU are a beautiful child of God. You are greatly loved and highly favored by God! God is not finished with you yet.

In 2015, my husband was diagnosed with non-Hodgkin's Lymphoma. The following pages are excerpts from a prayer book that I published, documenting my prayer journey as I trusted God for a complete eradication of cancer! Today, my husband is cancer-free! May you be blessed and encouraged as you believe God for MIRACLES!

Spiritual Warfare
Destroying The Spirit of Cancer

Cancer at its root is the result of human microbiological processes and structures having come under satanic attack. Cancer is a demonic adulteration of your body's natural processes. Cancer must be destroyed in prayer.

Spiritual Mapping

"For this purpose, the Son of God was manifested, that he might destroy the works of the devil."

1 John 3:8b

How Cancer Forms in The Body

Before we begin to pray, let us look at how cancer forms in the body.

In the beginning, God created humankind in His likeness, the enemy hates humanity. From the beginning Satan has been at work to destroy the marvelous beauty of God's design. Cancer at its root is the result of human microbiological processes and structures having come under satanic attack.

In the past, cancer has been a mysterious disease that resided somewhere in our body. Today, we understand the genetic and biological processes that are involved in the development and sustainment of cancer in the body. Since we understand how our genetic and biological processes are causing vulnerabilities, we can pray specifically for the systems of our bodies to operate as God intended.

In combating cancer through prayer, we can target our prayers of God's protection at the microbiological level where the attack on our DNA composition and the systems and processes of our bodies has occurred.

In combating cancer through prayer, we must target the physical processes that are operating outside the limits, control and boundaries that God created in our bodies as a defense against these kinds of attacks. It is here that we need to focus our prayers: that our body's defense network, which God established to protect us from destruction do their work.

Cancer has a malicious intent. Cancer comes from the pits of hell. Cancer cells do not want to coexist with you in your body, they want to control and consume your body. The goal of cancer is not to inconvenience you. Cancer's purpose is to steal, kill, and destroy your life. Your goal should never be to "live with cancer." Cancer cells are enemies of your body's normal, healthy processes. Our goal is to rid our bodies completely of this destructive invader.

We win the battle against cancer in the spiritual dimension, as well as in the physical dimension with medical attention.

"We wrestle not against flesh and blood, but against principalities, against authorities, against the universal lords of this darkness, against spiritual powers of wickedness in the heavenlies."

Ephesians 6:10

The Master Builder

Rebellion is the root of all disobedience. Rebellion at the cellular level is the essence of cancer development.

In his groundbreaking book, One Renegade Cell: The Quest for the Origin of Cancer, medical researcher Robert Weinberg states that the body is *"a highly complex society of rather autonomous cells (p. 2). He goes on to say that the danger from cancer lies in the fact that there is an absence of a single overseeing master builder, which seems to put the whole enterprise at risk. His point is that the body's cells appear to act under their own control or under the influence of other cells, but not under any identifiable centralized control. Because of this lack of oversight and control, cells can run amuck without any accountability or correction."*

"...A house divided against itself cannot stand."

Matthew 12:25b

When healthy cells rebel and replicate uncontrollably, on their own, it creates the biological environment for cancer cells to develop and flourish. In prayer, we must command that which has rebelled in our bodies to come back into alignment and the obedience of the Master Builder (God our Father). *"I am fearfully and wonderfully made,"* {Psalm 139:14}; acknowledges the Master Builder's central role in our biological makeup.

Destroying The Spirit of Cancer
Atomic Prayer
Weapons of Mass Destruction

"For she said within herself, If I may but touch his garment, I shall be whole."

Mathew 9:21

1. **Combat Renegade/Rebellious Cell Growth -** Cancer cells are produced when the cell growth accelerator, which signals the body to produce normal healthy cells, becomes adulterated and over produces cells on their own. The cells become self-sufficient providing itself with its own growth signals ignoring the body's signal of "no-growth". These renegade cells continue to divide and multiply creating the atmosphere for cancer to develop.

Spiritual Warfare Prayers:

- Heavenly Father, Psalms 139:14, declares that I am fearfully and wondrously made. Before I was formed in my mother's womb you knew me and saw every intricate detail involved in my physical, emotional, psychological, and physiological development. In Jesus' name, I ask that you bring perfect balance to my genetic make-up and to every system in my body.

- In Jesus' name and by His shed Blood, I destroy all rebellion that has taken place in the cellular replication and cellular inhibition processes in my body, and I bring these processes under the authority of Jesus, my Lord and Savior.

- In the name of Jesus and by His shed Blood, I cancel every assignment of the enemy at work at the microbiological level in my body to produce renegade cell replication that thwart the proper and systematic function of the organs and systems in my body.

- In the name of Jesus and by His shed Blood, I confront and destroy the taproot of the rebellious nature of every renegade cell and all renegade cell growth in my body. I declare that I am wonderfully made by the Master Builder, Abba Father. I command every cell in my body to follow only the Master Builder's command to replicate, In Jesus' name.

- In the name of Jesus and by His shed Blood, I reverse and destroy the negative effects that renegade cell growth has on the cell replication process in my body, my organs, and the systems in my body.

- In the name of Jesus and by His shed Blood, I declare that every cell in my body is now under the Lordship of Jesus and every cell, organ, and system in my body now functions in the perfect systematic order that Lord God Almighty intended.

2. **Put On the Brakes** - The normal biological process of cell replication has two pedals: An <u>accelerator</u> and a <u>brake</u>. The brake pedal signals healthy cell growth when to stop producing. Cancer is developed when our cell growth accelerator ignores the signal of the cell growth inhibitor to stop producing cells. When the cell growth accelerator ignores the signal to stop replicating, our cells continue to replicate without accountability, producing renegade cells that create an environment for cancer.

Spiritual Warfare Prayers:

- In the name of Jesus and by His shed Blood, I command the proper, perfect, and systematic function of my body's cellular replication and inhibition processes. I declare that the cellular replication and inhibition process in my body now responds to the Lord's commanded design and lines up in orderly obedience to Jesus my Lord and Savior.

- In the name of Jesus and by His shed Blood, I declare that the cell-replication inhibitor process in my body functions properly to halt out-of-control cell replication. In the name of Jesus, I declare that the cell replication process in my body functions normally as God has intended.

3. **Combat Inflammation & Elevated Tissue Temperatures -** So how does inflammation lead to cancer? Inflammation provides a boiler plant environment for renegade cells to regenerate. When a tiny tumor starts growing from a few renegade cells, it drains oxygen and nutrients from the rest of your body - and as a tumor grows bigger, demand starts to overtake supply. These cancer cells release chemicals that weaken the immune system's ability to fight against renegade cells.

    Inflammation is also a fire starter for metastasis by producing chemicals that help tumor cells nibble through the molecules tethering them to surrounding organs.

    Once developed, a cancerous tumor forms blood vessels, which ferry in much-needed oxygen and nutrients that feed and develop the tumor. The devil has some nerve! At this stage, the body may begin to show outward manifestations of weakness and tiredness. However, you must prepare for victory. You must establish in your heart, that through this adversity you will set your affections on God.

Keep in mind that the enemy's strategy is to wear you out through this attack of cancer in your body. Resist all fear. Be steadfast in the Lord. Bathe yourself in the word of God, in worship, in praise, in prayer, and in supplication.

We live in a fallen world. When Adam and Eve rebelled in the Garden of Eden sickness and disease was introduced to humanity. Cancer originates from the pits of hell, yet, we have been redeemed by the Blood of Jesus. Abba has a plan for your life and that plan does not include cancer.

The Bible tells us in Deuteronomy 34:7 that when Abba called Moses home to his rest, his eyes did not grow dim, nor was his natural strength abated.

Faith is the currency of heaven. Therefore, I declare unto you, child of God that according to the Word of God, your eyes shall not grow dim, nor shall your natural strength be abated. According to your days, so shall your strength be. You shall finish well! You shall finish strong!

Scripture Verses:

"Nay, in all these things we are more than conquerors through him that loved us. For I am persuaded, that neither death, nor life, nor angels, nor principalities, nor powers, nor things present, nor things to come, nor height, nor depth, nor any

other creature, shall be able to separate us from the love of God, which is in Christ Jesus our Lord."

Romans 8:37-39

"I will bless the Lord at all times: his praise shall continually be in my mouth."

Psalms 34:1

"These things I have spoken unto you, that in me ye might have peace. In the world ye shall have tribulation: but be of good cheer; I have overcome the world."

John 16:33

"Since, then, you have been raised with Christ, set your hearts on things above, where Christ is, seated at the right hand of God. Set your minds on things above, not on earthly things."

Colossians 3:1-2

"And the LORD will take away from you all sickness, and will afflict you with none of the terrible diseases of Egypt which you have known..."

Deuteronomy 7:15

"He giveth power to the faint; and to them that have no might he increaseth strength.... But they that wait upon the LORD shall renew their strength; they shall mount up with wings as eagles; they shall run, and not be weary; and they shall walk, and not faint."

Isaiah 40:29-31

Spiritual Warfare Prayers:

- In the name of Jesus and by His Blood, I destroy all microbiological and cellular inflammation that creates an environment for cancerous formations to occur in my body.

- In the name of Jesus and by His shed Blood, I destroy the production of increased inflammatory tissue, abnormal tissue, and elevated tissue temperatures. I command the perfect, proper, systematic function of all tissue production and temperature regulation in my body.

- At the name of Jesus, every knee must bow. In the name of Jesus and by His shed Blood, I command cancer *{name specific cancerous infiltration}* to leave my body now in the name of Jesus my salvation.

- In Jesus' name, and by His shed Blood, I cut off the life, the blood supply, oxygen, and nutrients to every tumor, malignant mass, malignant tissue, and abnormal growth that has developed in my body. I prohibit the formation of blood vessels that attribute to the feeding of cancerous cells, tumors and growths in my body. I command these abnormalities to eradicate and leave my body now in Jesus' name.

- In the name of Jesus and by His shed Blood, I command all cancer cells that have infected my blood cells, lymph nodes, organs, tissues, and the systems of my body, be flushed out of my body by the cleansing Blood of Jesus. I decree total divine restoration and repair to my body from the crown of my head to the soles of my feet. In Jesus' Name.

4. **Combat Tissue Invasion and Metastasis** - Tissue invasion and metastasis occur when cancer cells migrate across boundaries. Metastasis occurs when cancer cells break free of the primary tumor and spread to other organs.

Spiritual Warfare Prayers:

- In the name of Jesus and by His shed Blood, I destroy cancer from every cell, tissue, organ, and system in my body. In Jesus' name, I cut-off and prohibit the growth, spread, movement, migration, and metastasis of cancer in all its forms from operating in my body.

- In the name of Jesus; cancer I cut-off your blood supply, your oxygen, and your nutrients. I command you to dissipate and leave my body. In Jesus' name I eradicate, arrest, bind, destroy, and cast out all evidence and traces of cancer from every organ, cell, molecule, microbe, tissue, and micro tissue in my body.

- In Jesus' name and by His shed Blood, I activate the proper, perfect, and systematic function of my immune system, which Abba created to defend itself against sickness, disease, free-radicals and renegade cell growth. I declare that the defenses that God has built into my body to protect me from destruction will be strengthened to do their work efficiently and effectively without hindrance or compromise NOW in Jesus' name.

5. **Combat The Evasion of Apoptosis - When Cancer Cells Refuse to Degenerate.** Apoptosis is the opposite of cell growth; it is cell degeneration. Apoptosis is the natural process that cells go through where old cells degenerate and new cells are developed.

However, the evasion of apoptosis is the process when renegade cells divide and mutate uncontrollably and refuse to degenerate. A cancer cell not only hijacks normal cellular growth pathways but also prevents the natural cellular degeneration pathways.

Spiritual Warfare Prayers:

- In the name of Jesus and by His shed Blood, I cancel every assignment of the enemy that has come against the physical processes of my body to create and produce healthy tissue and cells. I cancel the assignment of renegade cells that are operating outside their limits, controls, boundaries, and lifespan. I annihilate all renegade cells that have divided and mutated uncontrollably causing cancer to form in my body.

- In the name of Jesus and by His shed Blood, the Blood of Jesus flushes my body of all cancer cells. The Blood of Jesus was shed for me. Blood for blood. Cell for cell. Molecule for molecule.

- In the name of Jesus, I activate the Blood of Jesus to eradicate all cancer from my body now in the name of Jesus. I cancel the assignment of renegade cells that have hijacked the normal cellular growth pathways and cellular degeneration (apoptosis) pathways in my body. I command these pathways to return to the proper, perfect, systematic order in which Abba has designed.

6. **Combat Sustained Angiogenesis** - Sustained angiogenesis occurs when adulterated blood vessels develop and mature. These blood vessels feed and give life to cancerous tissue, tumors, and masses.

Spiritual Warfare Prayers:

In the name of Jesus and by His shed Blood, I cut off the blood vessels, the blood supply, oxygen, and nutrients that feed and give life to cancerous cells, tissues, tumors, and masses in my body. I command these cancerous invaders to degenerate and leave my body in the name of Jesus.

7. **Combat Cancer's Replicative Potential** - Renegade cancer cells have the ability to reproduce and to mutate - stop them in their tracks!

Spiritual Warfare Prayers:

- The name of JESUS is above ALL names and ALL things. That includes cancer! Cancer in the name of Jesus and by His shed blood I command you to GO! In the name of Jesus, I activate the Blood of Jesus, to wipe out cancer and all evil diseases from my body. The Blood of Jesus is my receipt that the power of death, hell, the grave, cancer, sickness, disease, and all infirmities has been destroyed on Calvary; therefore, cancer has NO power or authority in my life. I command you to GO NOW and I prohibit your return.

- In the name of Jesus, by the power of the Blood of Jesus, I cancel the assignment of all metastases, re-occurrence, set-backs, regression, mutation, re-lapse, resistance, side effects from chemo-therapy treatments, and all forms of evil retaliation against my body. In the name of Jesus, my body is for the Lord and the Lord is for my body. Therefore, in the name of Jesus, Satan I command you to take your hands of my body NOW in the name of JESUS – AMEN!

"But he answered and said, every plant, which my Heavenly Father hath not planted, shall be rooted up."

Matthew 15:13

- Father, let these prayers be like <u>divine</u> atomic weapons of mass destruction that demolish their targets. Let every demon released from its assignment become a part of Jesus' footstool. We cancel every assignment of retaliation with the Word, the Blood, and the Spirit. Let every assignment of retaliation fail.

  In the Mighty Name of JESUS!

Kenyette Spencer

Atomic Prayer
For Divine Health
Weapons of Mass Destruction

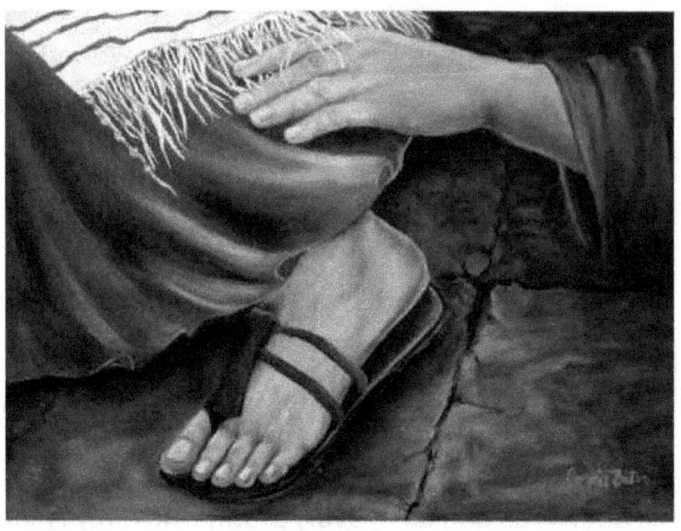

"But to you that fear my name shall the Sun of righteousness arise with healing in his wings; and you shall go forth and grow up as calves of the stall."

Malachi 4:2

Divine health is the will of God for our lives. As children of God, each stage of life is a welcomed journey. Almighty God governs our existence. Even as we age, we do not have to decline in vibrancy, strength, stamina, and health. Even our golden years can be the best years of our lives.

"His flesh shall be fresher than a child's: he shall return to the days of his youth: He shall pray unto God, and he will be

favourable unto him: and he shall see his face with joy: for he will render unto man his righteousness."

Job 33:25-26

"He giveth power to the faint; and to them that have no might he increaseth strength. Even the youths shall faint and be weary, and the young men shall utterly fall: But they that wait upon the LORD shall renew their strength; they shall mount up with wings as eagles; they shall run, and not be weary; and they shall walk, and not faint."

Isaiah 40:29-31

- In the name of Jesus, I declare that we prosper; we are in perfect health, even as our souls prosper. Lord, renew our youth, our vim, vigor, vitality, vibrancy, stamina, strength, energy, and beauty.

- In the name of Jesus, Lord, let our sleep be restorative and allow healing to take place as we sleep.

- In the name of Jesus, Lord, set me free from unforgiveness, bitterness, offense, resentment, and anything that would hinder your healing power in my life.

- In the name of Jesus, I plead the Blood of Jesus over my life, and ask that you protect me Lord from viruses, outbreaks, and epidemics. Lord, protect me from even the common cold and flu.

- In the name of Jesus, I plead the Blood of Jesus over our emotions. Lord, apply your oil and wine to the wounded places in our soul. Lord, bring health and healing to our minds, bodies, emotions, souls, and spirit so that we can live a healthy and well-balanced life in you.

- In the name of Jesus, I plead the blood of Jesus over every function of our bodies. We receive supernatural divine health. Holy Spirit, You are the creative power of GOD which moves over our bodies and destroys all illnesses in our bodies. Lord, please bring correction, balance, restoration, and healing to every function of our bodies, in JESUS' name.

- In the name of Jesus, I plead the blood of Jesus over our **Circulatory System**. I command the proper, perfect, and systematic function in the pumping and channeling of blood throughout the body using the lungs, heart, blood, and blood vessels.

- In the name of Jesus, I plead the blood of Jesus over our **Digestive System**. I command the proper, perfect, and systematic function in digesting and processing food with salivary glands, esophagus, stomach, liver, gallbladder, pancreas, intestines, colon, and rectum.

- In the name of Jesus, I plead the blood of Jesus over our **Endocrine System**. I command the proper, perfect, and systematic function of the communication processes within our bodies using hormones made by the endocrine glands, such as, the hypothalamus, pituitary gland, pineal gland, thyroid, parathyroids, and adrenals, and adrenal glands.

- In the name of Jesus, I plead the blood of Jesus over our **Excretory/Urinary System**. I command the proper, perfect, and systematic function of our kidneys, ureters, bladder, and urethra involved in fluid balance, electrolyte balance, and the excretion of urine.

- In the name of Jesus, I plead the blood of Jesus over our **Immune System & Lymphatic Systems**. I command the proper, perfect, and systematic function of structures involved in the transfer of lymph between tissues and the blood stream, the lymph and the nodes, and all transporting vessels that work together with our white blood cells, tonsils, adenoids, thymus, and spleen to defend against disease-causing agents.

- In the name of Jesus, I plead the blood of Jesus over our **Integumentary System** which regulates our skin, hair, and nails. I command the proper, perfect, and systematic function that would promote and maintain healthy, supple, flawless, beautiful, and youthful skin, hair, and nails.

- In the name of Jesus, I plead the blood of Jesus over our **Muscular System**. I command the proper, perfect, and systematic function over our muscular system which regulates our movement and muscles.

- In the name of Jesus, I plead the blood of Jesus over our **Nervous System**. I command the proper, perfect, and systematic function in collecting, transferring, and processing information with the brain, spinal cord, and nerves in the nervous system.

- In the name of Jesus, I plead the blood of Jesus over our **Reproductive System**. I command the proper, perfect, and systematic function of our reproductive organs.

- In the name of Jesus, I plead the blood of Jesus over our **Respiratory System** which regulates the organs used for breathing, the pharynx, larynx, trachea, bronchi, lungs and diaphragm. I command the proper, perfect, and systematic function of our respiratory System in Jesus' name.

- In the name of Jesus, I plead the blood of Jesus over our **Pulmonary System** which circulates blood to and from the heart and lungs. I command the proper, perfect, and systematic function of our pulmonary system in Jesus' name.

- In the name of Jesus, I plead the blood of Jesus over our **Skeletal System** and the structural support and protection of bones, cartilage, ligaments, and tendons in Jesus' name. In the name of Jesus, I plead the Blood of Jesus over our brain functions. I command the proper, perfect, and systematic function of all our brain functions which include:

    - **Occipital Lobe** (vision)
    - **Parietal Lobe** (senses)
    - **Temporal Lobe** (hearing, memory, speech, behavior)

- **Right Hemisphere** (creativity)
- **Left Hemisphere** (logic)
- **Corpus Callosom** (connects right and left hemispheres)
- **Cerebellum** (balance, posture, cardiac, respiratory)
- **Brain Stem** (movement and sensory)
- **Hypothalamus** (mood and motivation)
- **Thalamus** (sensory and motor functions)
- **Optic Chasm** (vision and optic nerves)
- **Pituitary Gland** (hormonal body processes)
- **Limbic System** (emotions)
- **Spinal Cord** (transmits signals to the brain)
- **Reticular Formation** (awake/sleep cycle)

- In the name of Jesus, Father we ask that you destroy every assignment of the enemy that would keep us in bondage:
    - Generational Curses
    - Ancestral Eccentricities / Peculiarities
    - Spirits of fear / Suspicions / Paranoia / Accusation
    - Pathological Conditions of the Mind/Body
    - Oddities / Inferiorities / Inadequacies
    - Emotional Delays / Arrested Development

- Habits / Personality Traits / Tendencies
- Ideologies / Perceptions / Mindsets / Ungodly Beliefs
- Disorders / Deficits / Impairments / Learning Disabilities
- Temperaments / Chemical Imbalances
- Physical Illnesses / Mental Illnesses / Emotional Imbalance
- Psychological Imbalances / Hormonal Imbalances

- In the name of Jesus, Father, re-generate {re-gene} our DNA and destroy every spirit of inheritance and predisposition to illnesses and diseases at the microbiological level.

- In the name of Jesus, Father, destroy all malfunctions /corruptions/ alterations/ and influences that alter, suppress, oppress, and repress our God given purpose, destiny, personality, and abilities: Spiritually, Emotionally, Psychologically, Neurologically, Economically, Socially, and Professionally. Lord, we ask you to bring us to the place of ultimate balance in you.

- Father, let these prayers be like <u>divine</u> atomic weapons of mass destruction that demolishes their target. Let every demon released from its assignment become a part of Jesus' footstool. We cancel every assignment of retaliation with the Word, the Blood, and the Spirit. Let every assignment of retaliation fail.

    In Jesus' Name – Amen!

Kenyette Spencer

Atomic Prayer
Combating Premature Death
Weapons of Mass Destruction

The Human Lifecycle

Combating Premature Death

"The thief cometh not, but for to steal, and to kill, and to destroy; I am come that they might have life, and that they might have it more abundantly."

John 10:10

Natural death is a part of the human life cycle. In God's order of things, as His children, we pass from death to eternal life with God. All humanity will experience the human lifecycle that God has ordained. However, premature death is not natural; it is an attack of the enemy against our lives that we must cancel in prayer. Premature death snatches mothers and fathers from their children. Premature death dashes our hopes and dreams against the rocks of despair. Premature death leaves unfinished work and thwarted destinies.

> *"For in death there is no remembrance of thee: in the grave who shall give thee thanks?"* Psalms 6:5

We live in a fallen world. Bad things do happen to good people. We have all lost someone too soon. The enemy comes to steal, to kill, and destroy our families and destinies. I lost my father when I was very young. I felt that void my entire life. Yet, God's grace makes up the difference when we have suffered loss.

When a child of God has finished their work on this earth, the transition from this world to eternity can be a welcomed transition that is accompanied with ease, peace, and much grace.

> *"But now Christ is risen from the dead and has become the firstfruits of those who have fallen asleep. For since by man came death, by Man also came the resurrection of the dead. For as in Adam all die, even so in Christ all shall be made alive. But each one in his own order: Christ the firstfruits, afterward those who are Christ's at His coming.*
> *Then comes the end, when He delivers the kingdom to God the Father, when He puts an end to all rule and all authority and power. For He must reign till He has put all enemies under His feet. The last enemy that will be destroyed is death.*
>
> 1 Corinthians 15:20-26

The Bible tells us in Deuteronomy 34:7, when God called Moses home to his rest, his eyes did not grow dim, nor was his natural strength abated. Therefore, according to our days, so shall our strength be. When God calls us home, we can go home in health; we do not have to go home in sickness. We can finish strong! We can finish well!

Kenyette Spencer

Atomic Prayer Against Premature Death Weapons of Mass Destruction

"I will deliver this people from the power of the grave; I will redeem them from death."

Hosea 13:14a

"I am he that liveth, and was dead; and, behold, I am alive for evermore, Amen; and have the keys of hell and of death."

Revelations 1:18

- Father, thank you for exempting me from every form of destruction, and for not allowing me to see evil in Jesus' name.

- Father, revoke every agreement, every contract, every covenant, and every decree of death concerning my life in Jesus' name.

- Father, delete my name from the enemy's list of destinies appointed to die suddenly and prematurely this year and beyond in Jesus' name.

- Every power pursuing my life for evil, fail with speed in Jesus' name.

- Every event and occurrences that leads to untimely death will not happen to me in the name of Jesus.

- Every root and seed of affliction in my body be uprooted now, by fire in Jesus' name.

- Assignment of untimely death assigned to waste my life, be destroyed in Jesus' name.

- My body hear the word of the Lord, reject every offer of sickness and affliction in Jesus' name.

- Power of God for divine protection and safety come upon me now in Jesus' name.

- I shall live and not die to declare the works of the Lord in the land of the living in Jesus' name.

- I rejoice for the Lord has rescued me from the hands of the destroyer in Jesus' name.

- I refuse to make any mistake that will give room to untimely death in my life in Jesus' name.

- Anything I will say or do that will open doors for sudden death in my life and family, I receive the grace not to say or do it in Jesus' name.

- Every trap of untimely death prepared for me, be destroyed by fire in the name of Jesus.

- I refuse to be a victim of evil manipulated accidents designed to lead to sudden death in Jesus' name.

- I refuse to die an untimely death due to sickness in Jesus' name.

- Every secret arrangement of darkness to terminate my life untimely be exposed and destroyed in Jesus' name.

- I take cover under the shadow of the Almighty from every destiny destroying force in Jesus' name.

- I rebuke every spirit of fear packaged to lead to my untimely death in Jesus' name.

- Father, thank you for frustrating the counsel of the wicked concerning me in Jesus' name.

- Thou agent of wickedness on assignment to attack my life with death, roast to ashes by the fire of God in Jesus' name.

- Every attack of the attackers to afflict me with sickness; roast to ashes in the name of Jesus.

- Father, destroy the enemy's assignment of death over my life in Jesus' name.

- Father, destroy every image and every dream of death, penury, and failure that the enemy has portrayed concerning me in Jesus' name.

- My body, hear the word of the Lord, refuse to cooperate with sickness in Jesus' name.

- Thou power of the grave lose your grip over my life in the name of Jesus.

- Cancer, come out of my body in the name of Jesus. My body is a no-go area for you! For the Lord is for my body and my body is for the Lord in Jesus' name.

- Every power of the grave speaking death over my life be silenced in Jesus' name.

- Blood of Jesus, speak against every life consuming force in operation to take my life in Jesus' name.

- Thank you, Lord, for securing your hand of protection upon my life and the lives of my family in Jesus' name.

- I receive the mark of "touch not" and an exemption from every evil disease in Jesus' name.

- Father, let these prayers be like <u>divine</u> atomic weapons of mass destruction that demolish their targets. Let every demon released from its assignment become a part of Jesus' footstool. We cancel every assignment of retaliation with the Word, the Blood, and the Spirit. Let every assignment of retaliation fail.

In Jesus' Name – Amen!

About the Author

Kenyette Spencer

Kenyette Spencer is a multi-disciplinary content creator. She is the creator of two internationally recognized web devotionals TheGodblog.org and Parasha with Passion.

Additionally, Kenyette is the author of a cookbook and lifestyle blog "Soul Food Is Food Made with Love."

Kenyette is the author of Combating Cancer through Prayer, which is a prayer guide that has encouraged many to find strength in God through their battle with cancer.

Kenyette specializes in helping others cultivate a life filled with beauty, inspiration, passion, and deep devotion with God. As an inspirational lifestyle blogger, Kenyette creates content that helps others experience their best life in God.

Kenyette is a student at Liberty University and is pursuing her ministry goal as a Chaplain. Kenyette, a Civil War historian, illuminates the experiences of free and enslaved individuals in the Shenandoah Valley during the Battle of Cedar Creek, sharing their stories with her community through historical interpretation. Kenyette enjoys flower gardening and resides in the Blue Ridge Mountains of Virginia.